AUTHENTIC
INDIAN COOKERY

AUTHENTIC INDIAN COOKERY

Shelina Jetha

RIGHT WAY

Typeset in 11/12pt Times by County Typesetters, Margate, Kent.
Printed and bound in Great Britain by Cox & Wyman Ltd., Reading, Berkshire.

The *Right Way* series and the *Paperfronts* series are both published by Elliot Right Way Books, Brighton Road, Lower Kingswood, Tadworth, Surrey, KT20 6TD, U.K.

CONTENTS

DEDICATION

If there is any one person to whom I would dedicate this book, it would be to my mother, Rabia Jetha; but for her I would not have learnt to cook. She taught me to cook a variety of dishes from Indian to English.

I learnt to cook at the age of nine, by default! My family were thrown out of Uganda and lost all their possessions. When we came to Britain, my mother had to go out to work for the first time in her life. Being the eldest girl of five children I was automatically volunteered to do the cooking when Mum was too busy. I used to hate it, until I went away to university and got married. Cooking for friends and my husband, Salim Hussein, was enjoyable and, furthermore, teaching students to cook at the local college was gratifying.

So, 'thanks, Mum, for teaching me to cook'!

INTRODUCTION

You have probably heard many times from 'Indian cooks' that what they cook is nothing like the food you get in Indian restaurants! I, too, will guarantee that my recipes are nothing like those you may have eaten in your local high street restaurant. My recipes are as I, and many of my friends and relatives, cook in our own homes; they are very simple and easy to make.

I learned to cook from my mother from a very early age, but our culinary influences were wide and varied. My grandparents were born in India, in the state of Gujrat, and moved to East Africa (where both of my parents were born and raised) because it was thought to be the 'land of opportunity'. While in Africa many of the native dishes were adopted and 'Indianised', such as the Mandazi and Chugu Kasori. Also, I am Ismaili Muslim but some of my cooking methods are similar to those used by Hindus. This is because my ancestors were Hindus who had been converted to Islam but retained many of the Hindu traditions, tastes and cookery methods.

Ingredients and Availability

Most of the ingredients you will be using should be available in your local supermarket. However, some things like karelas, goovar, saravgo singh, gram flour, chapatti flour, gulab jamboo flour, hondwo flour, etc., may have to be obtained from specialist shops. It would be to your advantage to visit such shops. If you are not sure about any of the ingredients, just ask the grocers and most will be more than willing to help!

There is a glossary at the back of this book to explain some of the many ingredients that you will be using. To get the best results, always use fresh ingredients and try to obtain all the ingredients recommended.

Garam Masala

When a recipe requires garam masala, do not use the ready-made packets which can be bought at the supermarket. It is much better to make your own as follows:

seeds from 4 cardamom pods
2 black peppercorns
2 cloves
½ nutmeg, grated
1cm (½ inch) cinnamon stick

Grind all together into a powder and keep in an airtight tin.

There are different ways of making garam masala, with different spices from those I have recommended. To achieve the best result with my recipes use the spices I have listed, in the ratios given here.

Chillies and Mustard Seeds

Care must be taken when handling 'hot' spicy ingredients like chillies and chilli powder. Always wash your hands thoroughly after handling hot spices or spicy ingredients because they can cause a very nasty burning sensation on the skin which is easily transferred from the hands to other parts of the body.

Fresh chillies can be used with or without the seeds. If you want the hotness from the chillies then include the seeds but leave them out if all you require is a gentle flavouring. The chillies used can be either red or green, but should be of the 'hot' variety.

Watch out when adding mustard seeds to hot oil – they will pop like crazy! Make sure that the heat is turned down, or better still, take the pan off the heat to control the temperature of the oil and then add the mustard seeds before returning to the heat.

Pots and Utensils

What pans you should use will depend on what you are cooking. Always use a wide, large, deep pan for recipes such as Muthias, Biryani or for deep frying. For recipes which require a period in the oven, either for actual cooking or to finish off the cooking process, you will need to use a handle-free pan (or one that is designed to be used both on the hob and in the oven) or a deep, wide, large ovenproof dish such as a casserole dish.

Most of the utensils I use will be found in most kitchens, but to make things like Chapattis and Parathas it is better to get a *velan*, which is a thin rolling pin, and a flat heavy iron pan or a griddle. A *karai* (a wok) is particularly useful for deep frying.

Frying And Deep Frying

For best results when frying, use vegetable oil.

Where 'deep frying' is required, make sure that the pan is at least half to three quarters full of oil. The ingredients to be deep fried should be almost submerged in the oil. You can tell if the oil is hot enough by testing a small amount of the ingredients to be fried. Any oil that is used for deep frying need not be discarded after use, but can be re-used for making the saks. Doing this will, in fact, add more flavour to these dishes!

In some of the recipes, deep fried, golden brown onions are required (i.e. Biryani and Beef Kalio). The onions should be peeled, chopped and fried in hot oil. Make sure you use a deep pan and be careful that the onions do not cause the oil to froth and spill over. To prevent this, only fry a handful at a time. The onions should look as if they are nearly burnt (i.e. a dark golden brown colour) and be crispy when cool.

Dry Cooking

In some recipes (i.e. Samosas and Bateta Chops) I suggest in the method that you 'dry cook' the meat. This means that the meat is cooked without any oil or other liquid. The meat should be cooked on a high heat and stirred frequently until it turns brown. The fat in the meat itself aids the process of cooking and for these recipes the final mixture needs to be as dry as possible, which is why no liquid is added.

Meat and Fish

Where the recipe requires minced meat you have the

option of using either lamb or beef, but make sure it is of good quality and does not have a high fat content. (However, for the Meat Samosa you can mince the breast of a chicken if you prefer.)

Where the recipe specifies the use of fish steaks, any kind and any size can be used, according to taste and appetite.

Whole Spices
When you add the whole spices needed to give recipes the right flavours – such as cardamom pods, cinnamon sticks, cloves, peppercorns, chillies, etc. – they will not disinte-grate during cooking, so warn your guests to look out for these when eating such dishes. The whole spices can be eaten by those who are accustomed to their hotness, or set aside by those who are unaccustomed (or unadventur-ous).

Pre-heated Oven
Where recipes require a pre-heated oven, set the oven at 200°C, 400°F or gas mark 6 half an hour before placing the dish in the oven. Change the setting as required for the cooking process according to the recipe.

Grains
Grains such as rice, lentils, moong beans, etc., are best cooked after pre-soaking them in water. Make sure the grains are completely immersed in the water and not floating freely. After soaking for the required period (as per the recipe), drain off the water and use fresh water for the cooking process. The grains should be added to cold water and then brought to the boil. Allow to simmer until the grains have cooked (they will be tender to the touch).

If you use the dry grains of kidney beans, make sure you pre-soak them at least overnight and cook thoroughly before adding to the recipe (i.e. for about 40 minutes, until just soft and mushy). Alternatively you can use tinned, pre-cooked kidney beans if you prefer.

Sugar and Milk

Where I suggest the use of sugar (i.e in the syrup for the Jardo and Gulab Jamboos) it is best to use granulated white sugar. Also, be warned: melted sugar is very hot, so be careful not to splash yourself!

In some of the recipes such as that for Kheer, I suggest you use whole milk for the best result. By whole milk, I mean pasteurised full fat – Silver Top – milk. Where there is no specification, then either skimmed, semi-skimmed or pasteurised full fat milk may be used, according to your preference.

Quantities

The recipes should serve four to six people. However, the quantities eaten will depend on individual appetites and also whether several courses are cooked or just one main course.

Conclusion

I have included a section to give you an idea of how to create menus using the recipes in this book.

Indian cookery is fun and flexible. Practice makes perfect and the recipes are designed to give you a guideline. Once you feel confident . . . let your taste buds do the cooking.

So relax, enjoy the cooking and Bon Appétit!

SUGGESTED MENUS

Vegetarian

Menu 1

Starter: Bhajias and Foodino Chutney
                    (pages 28 and 100)
Main course: Peas & Potato Pilau (page 77)
Accompaniments: Raita and 'Mum's' Salad (pages 99
                    and 101)
Sweet: Fresh Mango, peeled, sliced and
                    chilled

Menu 2

Starter: Kheer and Puris (pages 22 and 88)
Main course: Potato Sak, Daal, Chapattis and rice
                    (pages 66, 71 and 86)
Accompaniments: Lemon & Green Chilli Pickle
                    (page 105)
Sweet: Gulab Jamboos (page 94)

Menu 3

Starter: Jardo (page 18)
Main course: Bhaji, Chapattis and Ringra Khichri
                    (pages 72, 86 and 74)
Accompaniments: Carrot Pickle and plain yoghurt
                    (page 104)
Sweet: Kulfi (page 92)

Menu 4

Starter: Seero (page 20)
Main course: Moong Sak, Chapattis and rice
                    (pages 67 and 86)
Accompaniments: Carrot Pickle and plain yoghurt
                    (page 104)
Sweet: Milk Sev (page 91)

Meat

Menu 1

Starter: Kebabs (page 29)
Main course: Meat Biryani (page 81–82)
Accompaniments: Raita, 'Mum's' Salad and poppadoms
(pages 99 and 101)
Sweet: Fruit Salad (page 93)

Menu 2

Starter: Lapsi and poppadoms (page 19)
Main course: Beef Kalio, Naan Bread and
Spiced Rice (pages 52, 85 and 79)
Accompaniments: Sambharo (page 102)
Sweet: Milk Sev (page 91)

Menu 3

Starter: Meat Samosas (page 26)
Main course: Kuku Paka, Plain Parathas and
Spiced Rice (pages 40, 87 and 79)
Accompaniments: Poppadoms
Sweet: Sweet Potato Pudding (page 95)

Menu 4

Starter: Bateta Chops (page 30)
Main course: Tandoori Chicken and Chinese-Style
Rice (pages 43 and 80)
Accompaniments: Poppadoms
Sweet: Sweet Potato Pudding (page 95)

Vegetarian, Meat and Fish

Menu 1

Starter:	Vegetable Samosas (pages 24–25)
Main course:	Muthias, Chapattis and Spiced Rice (pages 50–51, 86 and 79)
Accompaniments:	Poppadoms and Lemon & Green Chilli Pickle (page 105)
Sweet:	Gulab Jamboos (page 94)

Menu 2

Starter:	Hondwo (page 31–32)
Main course:	Kebab Sak, Plain Parathas and Spiced Rice (pages 54, 87 and 79)
Accompaniments:	Sambharo (page 102)
Sweet:	Fresh Pawpaw

Menu 3

Starter:	Lapsi (page 19)
Main course:	Fish Sak, Daal, Chapattis and Spiced Rice (pages 34–35, 71, 86 and 79)
Accompaniments:	'Mum's' Salad and Raita (pages 101 and 99)
Sweet:	Fruit Salad (page 93)

Menu 4

Starter:	Bhajias (page 28)
Main course:	Bhaji, Chapattis and Fish Pilau (pages 72, 86 and 36–37)
Accompaniments:	Sambharo (page 102)
Sweet:	Gulab Jamboos (page 94)

1

SWEET STARTERS

JARDO

This is a sweet rice dish made with exotic ingredients, for those with a very sweet tooth.

cooking time: 50 minutes   *serves:* 4
            + pre-soaking time

250g (9 oz) rice, washed and pre-soaked for ½ hour
½ tsp yellow food colouring
250ml (½ pt) water
150g (5 oz) granulated sugar
¼ tsp cardamom seeds
pinch of saffron
150g (5 oz) pineapple chunks
25g (1 oz) chopped dates (optional)
50g (2 oz) butter
5cm (2 inch) cinnamon stick
4 pods cardamom
25g (1 oz) sultanas
For decoration:
50g (2 oz) almonds and pistachios, coarsely chopped
desiccated coconut

1. Wash and soak the rice, then drain and boil for 35 minutes in fresh water with half the colouring. Drain.
2. In another saucepan put the 250ml (½ pt) water, the sugar, cardamom seeds, saffron and the rest of the colour and boil until a syrup forms and the liquid has almost reduced to half its quantity. (Be careful not to splash yourself as melted sugar is *very* hot.)
3. Add the pineapple and dates.
4. Add the rice to the syrup and mix until all the syrup has been absorbed by the rice.
5. In a separate pan, melt the butter, add the cinnamon, cardamom pods and sultanas.
6. Add all this to the rice and leave in a switched off hot oven (see introduction, page 11) for 20 minutes.
7. Decorate with the nuts and coconut.

Serving suggestion: Serve as a starter with shop bought poppadoms.

LAPSI

A delicious, sweet starter made with cracked wheat. This dish is cooked both on the hob and in the oven.

cooking time: 1 hour   *serves:* 6

50g (2 oz) butter
3 cardamom pods, opened
2.5cm (1 inch) cinnamon stick
115g (4 oz) cracked wheat (bulgar)
25g (1 oz) sultanas
125ml (¼ pt) milk
125ml (¼ pt) water
½ tsp ground nutmeg
½ tsp ground cinnamon
50g (2 oz) sugar
50g (2 oz) desiccated coconut
2 strands saffron
For decoration:
desiccated coconut

1. Melt the butter in a saucepan on low heat.
2. Add the whole spices and fry for 5 minutes.
3. Add the bulgar wheat, fry for 10–15 minutes, until golden brown, and keep stirring.
4. Add the sultanas and fry for a minute, until they swell.
5. Add the rest of the ingredients, keep stirring and bring to the boil.
6. Cover (or transfer to a lidded ovenproof dish, if necessary) and put in the oven (180°C, 350°F or gas mark 4), and cook for another 35–40 minutes, until it appears fluffy.
7. Sprinkle with desiccated coconut before serving.

Serving suggestion: Serve hot with shop bought poppadoms.

SEERO
A sweet starter made with semolina and spices.

cooking time: 1 hour   *serves:* 4

85g (3 oz) butter
115g (4 oz) semolina
25g (1 oz) sultanas
1 tsp ground nutmeg
1 tsp ground cinnamon
50g (2 oz) sugar
125ml (¼ pt) milk
125ml (¼ pt) evaporated milk
2 strands saffon
water, as required
For decoration:
handful almonds, coarsely ground
desiccated coconut

1. Melt the butter on low heat, add the semolina and fry for 20 minutes, stirring frequently.
2. Add the sultanas and fry for 5 minutes, until they swell.
3. Add the rest of the ingredients (except the water) and bring to the boil, stirring vigorously all the time.
4. Cover and simmer for 30 minutes and keep stirring frequently. If the mixture begins to dry up before the semolina has cooked add drops of water as required.
5. When the semolina has cooked, i.e. almost doubled in quantity, it is ready.
6. Before serving, sprinkle with nuts and desiccated coconut.

Serving suggestion: Serve hot, alongside a savoury starter.

SEV

A sweet starter made with vermicelli and spices.

cooking time: 40 minutes   *serves:* 4–6

115g (4 oz) butter
4 cardamom pods, opened
2.5cm (1 inch) cinnamon stick
150g (5 oz) vermicelli
115g (4 oz) sultanas
1 tsp ground nutmeg
1 tsp ground cinnamon
250ml (½ pt) water
For decoration:
desiccated coconut

1. Melt the butter on low heat, add the whole spices and fry for 5 minutes.
2. Scrunch the vermicelli and add to the butter and fry for 10 minutes until golden brown.
3. Add the sultanas and fry for a few minutes, until they swell.
4. Add the rest of the ingredients and bring to the boil.
5. Cover and simmer for 25 minutes, until all the water has been absorbed and the vermicelli is tender to touch.
6. Sprinkle with desiccated coconut before serving.

Serving suggestion: This tastes delicious with bhajias.

KHEER

A sweet starter made with rice and spices.

cooking time: 1 hour 20 minutes   *serves:* 4–6
                  + pre-soaking time

85g (3 oz) rice, washed and soaked for 30 minutes
50g (2 oz) butter
4 cardamom pods, opened
2.5cm (1 inch) cinnamon stick
50g (2 oz) sultanas
500ml (1 pt) full fat milk
50g (2 oz) sugar
1 tsp ground cinnamon
1 tsp ground nutmeg
pinch of saffron
water, as required

1. Wash and soak the rice, then drain it.
2. Melt the butter and add the whole spices and sultanas and fry for at least 5 minutes.
3. Add the milk and the rest of the ingredients, EXCEPT for the rice and water, and bring to the boil.
4. Add the rice and boil for a further 5 minutes.
5. Cover and simmer for 40 minutes, until the rice is mushy to touch. Add some water if the mixture begins to dry up.

N.B. The consistency of this dish should be like rice pudding.

Serving suggestions: Serve hot with puris, parathas or chapattis.

SAVOURY STARTERS

VEGETABLE SAMOSA

A triangular pastry with a vegetable filling and deep fried until golden brown.

cooking time: 1 hour   *serves:* 6

For the filling:
2 tbsp oil
2 medium sized onions, finely chopped
    OR 2 bunches of spring onions, finely chopped
4 tsp crushed garlic
4 tsp grated ginger
115g (4 oz) finely cubed potatoes
115g (4 oz) finely cubed carrots
50g (2 oz) peas
3 or more green chillies, finely chopped
handful of chopped coriander
2 tsp garam masala powder
1 tsp turmeric powder
juice of 1 lemon
chilli powder to taste
salt to taste
63ml (⅛ pt) water
oil for deep frying
For the paste:
2 tbsp plain flour
water for binding
For the pockets:
20 Samosa pastry strips

1. Heat the oil and add the onions.
2. When the onions have softened, add the garlic and ginger and fry for 5 minutes.
3. Then add all the other ingredients (except for the oil for deep frying), cover and simmer for 40 minutes until all the vegetables have gone mushy. Allow to cool.
4. Prepare a thick paste with the flour and water.
5. Fold the pastry into a triangular pocket (see diagram following) and fill with the vegetable mixture.
6. Seal the pocket flaps with the flour paste.

7. Heat the oil and fry each samosa until golden brown and drain on kitchen paper towels.

Serving suggestion: Serve as a starter with salad, a wedge of lemon and a dip or chutney.

FOLDING A SAMOSA

Samosa pastry comes in circles. You need to cut them into three strips and then fold these strips into triangles, and fill and seal them as follows:

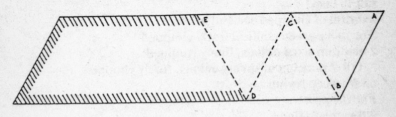

Key: area to edge with flour and water paste to seal the samosa

1. Fold along line BC, taking point A to D.
2. Next, fold along line CD, taking point B to E.
3. Having created this pocket, hold it loosely in your hand and fill with the samosa mixture, making sure that AB is lying flat to CE.
4. Dab the free edges with a flour and water paste and wrap the loose flap of pastry around the triangle to seal the pocket completely.
5. Dab a little flour and water paste over any gaps or holes in the pastry pocket.

NOTE: if there are any holes the samosa will become oil logged and lose its filling as well as its taste during frying.

(If you are new to folding samosas it may help you to fold a strip of paper as per the directions before trying with the pastry strips.)

MEAT SAMOSA

A triangular pastry filled with minced meat and deep fried
until golden brown.

cooking time: 1 hour   *serves:* 6

For the filling:
300g (11 oz) mince
4 tsp crushed garlic
4 tsp grated ginger
2 tsp garam masala powder
salt to taste
handful of chopped coriander
3 or more green chillies, finely chopped
2 medium sized onions, finely chopped
    OR 2 bunches of spring onions, finely chopped
oil for deep frying
For the paste:
2 tbsp plain flour
water for binding
For the pockets:
20 Samosa pastry strips

1. Dry cook the mince (i.e. without any oil) in a non-stick
   pan.
2. Add the garlic, ginger, garam masala and salt and stir.
3. Take off heat, allow to cool, add the coriander, chillies
   and onions.
4. Prepare a thick paste with the flour and water.
5. Fold the pastry into a triangle pocket (see preceding
   diagram) and fill with the mince mixture.
6. Seal the pocket flaps with the flour paste.
7. Heat the oil and fry the samosa until golden brown and
   drain on kitchen paper towels.

N.B. Wash hands thoroughly after handling chillies.

*Serving suggestion: Serve as a starter with salad, a wedge of
lemon and a dip or chutney.*

BATETA WARA
These are a type of potato fritter.

cooking time: 1 hour   *serves:* 6

450g (1 lb) potatoes, boiled and mashed
4 tsp crushed garlic
4 tsp grated ginger
1 tsp turmeric powder
1 tsp chilli powder
handful of coriander leaves, chopped
juice of 1 lemon
salt to taste
oil for deep frying
For batter:
115g (4 oz) gram flour
125ml (¼ pt) water
pinch of salt
½ tsp chilli powder

1. *For the potato balls:* mix all the ingredients (EXCEPT the oil) with the mashed potatoes.
2. Roll into equal sized balls (actual size depending on your preference).
3. *For the batter:* mix all the ingredients together.
4. Heat the oil for frying.
5. Dip the balls into the batter then deep fry until golden brown and drain on kitchen paper towels.

Serving suggestions: Serve hot with some ambli or tomato ketchup.

BHAJIAS

Fritters, also known as 'onion bhajis'. However, these are made with any vegetable of your choice e.g. sliced potatoes, aubergines or mushrooms; cauliflower heads; sliced capsicum peppers; green chillies split lengthwise, etc.

cooking time: 40 minutes   *serves:* 4

150g (5 oz) gram flour
1 tsp celery seeds (ajma)
1 tsp cumin seeds
4 tsp crushed garlic
2 tsp grated ginger
¼ tsp baking powder
1 medium sized onion, sliced
handful of chopped fresh coriander and fenugreek leaves
1 small potato, finely sliced or coarsely grated
handful of other vegetables of your choice
1 tsp salt (or to taste)
water
oil for deep frying

1. Mix all the ingredients (EXCEPT the oil) with small amounts of water until a batter of dropping consistency is formed.
2. Heat the oil for frying and add a tablespoon of this hot oil to the batter mixture.
3. Take a tablespoon of the batter and fry until golden brown.
4. Drain on kitchen paper towels.

N.B. Wash hands thoroughly after handling chillies.

Serving suggestions: Serve as a starter with a dip or chutney.

KEBABS

A special mixture of minced meat and spices makes this a mouth-watering dish!

cooking time: 1 hour 30 minutes   *serves:* 4–6

500g (1 lb 2 oz) mince
2 medium sized onions, coarsely grated or finely sliced
4 slices bread, crumbled
4 green chillies, finely chopped
handful of finely chopped coriander
4 tsp grated ginger
4 tsp crushed garlic
2 tsp garam masala
1 large egg
juice of ½ lemon
salt to taste
oil for deep frying

1. Mix together all the ingredients (EXCEPT the oil) and marinate for at least 1 hour.
2. Roll into small balls (kebabs), deep fry until golden brown and drain on kitchen paper towels. Alternatively, cook under a hot grill, turning frequently.

N.B. Wash hands thoroughly after handling chillies.

Serving suggestion: Serve as a starter with a wedge of lemon and salad.

BATETA CHOPS

A spicy mixture of minced meat folded in a pocket of mashed potato and fried until golden brown.

cooking time: 1 hour   *serves:* 6

250g (9 oz) mince
4 tsp crushed garlic
4 tsp grated ginger
salt to taste
1 tsp garam masala
2 medium sized onions, finely chopped
handful of chopped coriander leaves
4 green chillies, finely sliced
1kg (2 lb 2 oz) potatoes, peeled, boiled and mashed
oil for frying
For coating:
2 eggs
chilli powder to taste (optional)
breadcrumbs or semolina

1. Dry cook the meat, add the garlic, ginger and salt.
2. Take off the heat, add the garam masala, onions, coriander and chillies.
3. Take a handful of mashed potato and make a 'well' in the middle, fill with the meat mixture and roll into cakes (i.e. slightly flattened balls).
4. Whip the eggs and add some chilli powder if wanted.
5. Dip the cakes in the egg, then coat with breadcrumbs or semolina and fry until golden brown.
6. Drain on kitchen paper towels.

N.B. Wash hands thoroughly after handling chillies.

Serving suggestion: Serve as a starter with a lemon wedge, salad and/or ambli.

HONDWO

This is a vegetarian savoury cake, full of rich flavours and very delicious.

cooking time: 1 hour 30 minutes   *serves:* 6
              + standing time

200g (7 oz) Hondwo flour
115g (4 oz) rice flour
150g (5 oz) plain yoghurt
4 tsp crushed garlic
3 tsp grated ginger
50g (2 oz) semolina
50g (2 oz) gram flour
4 green chillies, finely chopped
handful finely chopped coriander leaves
1 tsp sugar
1 small carrot, coarsely grated
1 small potato, coarsely grated
1 medium sized onion, finely chopped
1 tbsp peas
handful finely shredded cabbage
1–2 tbsp lemon juice
salt to taste
hot water
3 tbsp oil
1 tsp cumin seeds
2 tsp black mustard seeds
6 curry leaves
1 tsp Eno salt
2 tsp sesame seeds

1. Put all the ingredients into a bowl EXCEPT for the oil, cumin and mustard seeds, curry leaves, Eno salt and sesame seeds.
2. Add enough hot water to mix into a thick paste, then allow to stand overnight or at least for 2 hours.
3. Heat the oil, add the cumin and mustard seeds and curry leaves.
4. When seeds start to pop, pour into mixture and stir.

5. Stir in the Eno salt.
6. Pour mixture into a well-greased baking tin and place in the oven (190°C, 375°F or gas mark 5).
7. After 30 minutes, sprinkle the top with sesame seeds.
8. Cook for another 40 minutes or until the top appears golden brown and when a skewer is inserted it comes out clean.

N.B. Wash hands thoroughly after handling chillies.

Serving suggestions: Serve hot or cold with yoghurt or ambli.

3

FISH & CHICKEN

FISH SAK

A very delicious, full flavoured dry curry, that does not mask the flavour of the fish.

cooking time: 1 hour 30 minutes   *serves:* 4
                    + marinading time

1kg (2 lb 2 oz) fish fillets, steaks or strips
For marinade:
4 tbsp coriander powder
1 tsp salt
Juice of ½ lemon
1 tsp chilli powder
For frying:
oil for deep frying
3 medium sized potatoes, cut into thick chips
For sauce:
3 tbsp oil
4 cloves
4 black peppercorns
1 large onion, sliced
2 tsp crushed garlic
2 tsp finely grated ginger
2 tbsp tomato purée
2 whole green chillies (optional)
400g (14 oz) peeled, chopped tomatoes
3 tsp coriander powder
¼ tsp turmeric powder
chilli powder to taste
salt to taste
water
fresh chopped coriander for garnish

1. Marinade the fish in a thick paste made of coriander power, salt, lemon juice and chilli powder for at least 40 minutes or overnight for the best result.
2. Deep fry the fish until golden brown and drain on kitchen paper towels or grill under a hot grill until golden brown.

3. Deep fry the chipped potatoes until golden brown and drain on kitchen paper towels.
4. *To make the sauce:* Heat oil, add cloves, peppercorns and onion. When the onion has browned add the garlic, ginger, tomato purée, green chillies, tomatoes, coriander powder, turmeric powder, chilli powder and salt to taste.
5. Stir and add drops of water to make the sauce into dropping consistency.
6. Let the sauce simmer on low heat for 20 minutes and keep stirring frequently.
7. Lay the fish and potato chips in an ovenproof dish and pour over the sauce.
8. Garnish with chopped coriander.
9. Heat through in a moderately hot oven (180°C, 350°F, gas mark 4) before serving.

N.B. Always wash hands thoroughly after handling chillies.

Serving suggestion: Serve hot as a main course with chapattis.

FISH PILAU

Savoury rice, great as a main meal or even for a buffet.

cooking time: 1 hour   *serves:* 4–6
                + pre-soaking time

450g (1 lb) rice, washed and soaked for 40 minutes
3 tbsp oil
1 large onion, sliced
2 tsp cumin seeds
3 cardamom pods
2 × 2.5cm (1 inch) cinnamon sticks
8 cloves
8 black peppercorns
4 tsp crushed garlic
4 tsp grated ginger
4 green chillies, whole or chopped
4 medium fish steaks, cut into chunks
115g (4 oz) prawns
150g (5 oz) peeled, chopped tomatoes
6 small potatoes, peeled and cut into quarters
250ml (½ pt) water
handful of chopped coriander leaves
salt to taste
25g (1 oz) butter or margarine

1. Wash and soak the rice.
2. Heat the oil and add the onion, cumin seeds, cardamom pods, cinnamon, cloves and peppercorns.
3. When the onion has softened, add the garlic, ginger
   and chillies and fry for 2 minutes.
4. Then add the fish, prawns, tomatoes, rice, potatoes
   and water, along with the chopped coriander leaves
   and salt to taste.
5. Bring to the boil and then cover and simmer on low
   heat for 40 minutes until the rice has cooked.
6. Add the butter or margarine in blobs, while hot.

N.B. To prevent rice from going mushy, never stir while it

is cooking.

Wash hands thoroughly after handling chillies.

Serving suggestion: Serve as a main course with 'Mum's' Salad, raita and pickles.

TANDOORI FISH

cooking time: 40 minutes   *serves:* 6
               + marinading time

6 fish steaks
3 tbsp tandoori powder
1 small carton plain yoghurt (150g)
3 tsp crushed garlic
3 tsp grated ginger
1 tsp salt
juice of one lemon
1 tsp chilli powder

1. Marinade the fish for at least 2 hours, or preferably overnight, in a mixture made of the above ingredients.
2. Cook in a pre-heated oven (190°C, 375°F, gas mark 5) for 40 minutes until the fish has cooked.

N.B. The fish has to be cooked on a flat baking tray for the tandoori colour and flavour to come through.

Serving suggestions: Serve as a starter or as a main course with chipped potatoes and salad.

KOORI FISH

This is a quicker way of cooking fish, with a slightly
different flavour.

cooking time: 40 minutes   *serves:* 6

3 tbsp oil
3 tsp coriander powder
1 tsp cumin powder
½ tsp turmeric powder
½ tsp chilli powder
2 tsp crushed garlic
1 tsp grated ginger
2 whole chillies
2 tsp tomato purée
150g (5 oz) peeled, chopped tomatoes
6 fish steaks
2 tsp salt (or to taste)
water, if necessary
handful of chopped coriander leaves for garnish

1. Heat the oil in a saucepan, add the powders and fry for
   3 minutes, stirring frequently.
2. Add the rest of the ingredients (EXCEPT the water and
   coriander leaves), stir for 2 minutes, cover and cook on
   low heat for 30 minutes until the fish flakes off easily.
   If it begins to dry out before the fish is done, add a
   drop of water to aid the cooking.
3. Garnish with the chopped coriander leaves before
   serving.

*Serving suggestions: Serve with some fried chipped pota-
toes and salad or with Daal, chapattis and rice.*

PRAWN SAK

This is a strong flavoured dish, where the flavour of the prawns and the sauce should come through.

cooking time: 40 minutes   *serves:* 4–6

2 tbsp oil
1 small onion, sliced
2 tsp crushed garlic
1 tsp tomato purée
50g (2 oz) peeled, chopped tomatoes
1 tsp coriander powder
¼ tsp turmeric powder
½ tsp chilli powder
200g (7 oz) prawns
salt to taste
water as required

1. Heat the oil and fry the onion until golden brown.
2. Then add the garlic and tomato purée and fry for 3 minutes.
3. Now add the rest of the ingredients, stir, cover and simmer for 30 minutes.
4. Add drops of water if the sauce becomes too dry.

Serving suggestion: Serve with Daal, chapattis and rice as a main course.

KUKU PAKA
A spiced chicken and coconut dish, full of exotic flavours!

cooking time: 50 minutes   *serves:* 4–6

800g (1 lb 12 oz) chicken pieces
5 green chillies, finely chopped
2 whole chillies
4 tsp crushed garlic
4 tsp grated ginger
250g (9 oz) peeled, chopped tomatoes
½ tsp turmeric powder
3 tbsp lemon juice
150g (5 oz) coconut cream
salt to taste
4 medium sized potatoes, cut into quarters
500ml (1 pt) water
1 large onion, sliced
4 hard boiled eggs (optional)
handful of chopped coriander leaves, for garnish

1. Put all the ingredients EXCEPT the eggs and coriander into a big saucepan.
2. Bring to the boil, lower the heat, cover and simmer for at least 50 minutes, until the chicken is cooked.
3. Add the eggs and garnish with chopped coriander leaves.

N.B. Wash hands thoroughly after handling chillies.
This dish can be re-heated, but do so gently.

Serving suggestion: Serve with chapattis and rice.

SPICY DRUMSTICKS

These are spicy chicken drumsticks which are deep fried until golden brown.

cooking time: 1 hour 30 minutes   *serves:* 6

12 chicken drumsticks
4 tsp crushed garlic
2 tsp grated ginger
4 cloves
4 black peppercorns
2.5cm (1 inch) cinnamon stick
3 cardamom pods
1 tsp cumin seeds
1 tsp turmeric powder
1 tsp chilli powder
2 tsp salt (or to taste)
500ml (1 pt) water
For the coating:
150g (5 oz) plain flour (and more if required)
1 tsp garam masala
¼ tsp turmeric powder
½ tsp chilli powder
½ tsp salt
3 eggs
oil for deep frying

1. Put the chicken drumsticks in a large saucepan with all the ingredients (EXCEPT the batter mixture), bring to the boil, cover and simmer for 40 minutes.
2. *For the coating:* Mix the plain flour with the garam masala, turmeric powder, chilli powder and salt in a deep bowl.
3. Whisk the eggs in a separate bowl.
4. Heat the oil in a large saucepan, coat the chicken drumsticks with the whisked egg, dip into the flour mixture and deep fry until golden brown. Drain on kitchen paper towels.

Serving suggestions: Serve hot as a starter or as an accompaniment with Chinese-style Rice.

RABIA CHICKEN
A dry, spicy chicken dish, eaten as a starter or as an accompaniment.

cooking time: 1 hour   *serves:* 4

2 tbsp oil
3 tsp crushed garlic
3 tsp grated ginger
4 tbsp tomato purée
2 tsp coriander powder
1 tsp chilli powder (or to taste)
¼ tsp turmeric powder
1 tbsp tikka powder
1 tsp salt
8 chicken legs or thighs

1. Heat the oil and add the garlic, ginger and tomato purée and fry for 4 minutes.
2. Add the rest of the ingredients and stir frequently for 10 minutes over a medium heat.
3. Transfer to a baking tray and cook in the oven (200°C, 400°F or gas mark 6) for 40 minutes until the chicken is tender.

Serving suggestions: Serve as a starter with raita and salad or as an accompaniment to a main course such as Peas & Potato Pilau.

TANDOORI CHICKEN

A common dish in Indian restaurants, this is rich flavoured and dry. It can be served as a starter or as a side dish with a main course.

cooking time: 1 hour   *serves:* 4–6
                      + marinading time

6 chicken pieces (thighs, quarters or legs)
1 small carton of plain yoghurt (150g)
4 tsp crushed garlic
4 tsp grated ginger
5 tbsp Tandoori powder
1 tsp chilli powder
1 tbsp oil
salt to taste

1. Make small slits in the chicken pieces and marinade them in a thick paste made up of all of the above ingredients for at least 2 hours, or preferably overnight.
2. Place the chicken pieces on a baking tray and cook in a pre-heated oven (180°C, 350°F or gas mark 4) for 50 minutes or until the chicken is cooked.
3. Then grill the pieces under a hot grill until they turn red.

Serving suggestions: Serve with lemon wedges, salad and/ or the Chinese-style Rice.

ROASTED SPICY CHICKEN
This is a 'Sunday roast' with a bit of spice!

cooking time: 1 hour 40 minutes   *serves:* 4–6

2 tbsp oil
2 tsp crushed garlic
2 tsp grated ginger
2 tsp tomato purée
150g (5 oz) peeled, chopped tomatoes
2 tsp coriander powder
¼ tsp turmeric powder
½ tsp chilli powder
1 tsp garam masala
2 tsp salt (or to taste)
1.4kg (3 lb) whole chicken, with giblets removed
handful of chopped coriander leaves for garnish

1. Heat the oil and add the garlic and ginger and fry for 2 minutes, stirring constantly.
2. Add the tomato purée and cook for another 2 minutes.
3. Then add the tomatoes, powders and salt and cook for 7 minutes, stirring frequently.
4. Make fine slits in the chicken and cover with the sauce.
5. Place the chicken on a baking tray and cook in the oven (190°C, 375°F or gas mark 5) for an hour and a half. The chicken is cooked when a skewer can be easily inserted in the chicken and the juices do not contain any blood.
6. Garnish with the chopped coriander leaves before serving.

Serving suggestions: Serve as a side dish with the Peas & Potato Pilau or simply with a baked potato and plain yoghurt.

4

MEAT & EGGS

MEAT SAK

The combination of spices makes this a very simple but effective dish.

cooking time: 1 hour   *serves:* 4–6

5 tbsp oil
8 cloves
8 black peppercorns
4 cardamom pods
2.5cm (1 inch) cinnamon stick
1 large onion, sliced
2 tsp grated ginger
2 tsp crushed garlic
2 tbsp tomato purée
250g (9 oz) peeled, chopped tomatoes
4 tsp coriander powder
¼ tsp turmeric powder
½ tsp chilli powder
1 tsp garam masala
2 whole green chillies, split in half lengthwise (optional)
salt to taste
800g (1 lb 12 oz) lamb or beef cubes
2 medium sized potatoes, cut into quarters
125ml (¼ pt) water or stock*
chopped coriander leaves to garnish

1. Heat the oil, add the whole spices and onion.
2. When the onion is golden brown, add the ginger and garlic and fry for 2 minutes.
3. Then add the tomato purée and fry for a further minute.
4. Add the tomatoes, powders, garam masala, chillies (if using) and salt. Stir.
5. Add the meat and potatoes. Stir.
6. Add 125ml (¼ pt) water, cover and simmer on low heat for 40 minutes until the meat is cooked. Keep checking to ensure the sauce is not drying up before the meat is cooked, and add more water if necessary.

7. Garnish with the chopped coriander.

N.B. Always wash hands thoroughly after handling chillies.

*The meat could be pre-cooked with a handful of chopped onion mixed with crushed garlic/ginger, a few cloves and peppercorns, cardamom, a small piece of cinnamon, 2 tsp of whole cumin seeds and 250ml (½ pt) water. The stock is then used to make the sauce instead of just water.

Serving suggestion: Serve as a main course with chapattis, rice and a salad.

GARLIC & GINGER STEAKS

These are luxurious and a delicious way of cooking steaks.

cooking time: 1 hour   *serves:* 6
              + marinading overnight (optional)

4 tsp crushed garlic
3 tsp grated ginger
3 crushed chillies
2 tsp garam masala
2 tsp salt
1 tsp ground black pepper
2 tbsp oil
6 × 170g (6 oz) steaks

1. Mix together the garlic, ginger, chillies, garam masala,
   salt, ground black pepper and the oil.
2. Cut fine slits in the steaks and rub the above mixture
   into them, on both sides.
3. Heat a grill on high and cook the steaks until they
   brown on both sides.

N.B. These taste even better if they are marinaded in the
above mixture overnight.
Wash hands thoroughly after handling chillies.

*Serving suggestion: Serve hot with fried, chipped potatoes
and ambli.*

KHEEMA SAK

Very easy to make, this is a mouth watering minced meat dish.

cooking time: 50 minutes   *serves:* 4–6

3 tbsp oil
1 large onion, sliced
4 cloves
4 cardamom pods, opened
6 black peppercorns
2.5cm (1 inch) cinnamon stick
2 tsp crushed garlic
2 tsp grated ginger
1 tbsp tomato purée
150g (5 oz) peeled, chopped tomatoes
½ tsp turmeric powder
½ tsp chilli powder
2 tsp coriander powder
3 medium sized potatoes, peeled and quartered
450g (1 lb) mince
125–250ml (¼–½ pt) water
salt to taste
handful of fresh coriander leaves, chopped, for garnish

1. Heat the oil and add the onion and whole spices.
2. When the onion has browned, add the garlic and ginger and fry for 3 minutes.
3. Then add the tomato purée and let it stand in the oil for at least 2 minutes before stirring.
4. Now add the rest of the ingredients (EXCEPT the coriander leaves), cover and simmer for 30 minutes, until the potatoes and mince have cooked.
5. Garnish with chopped coriander leaves before serving.

Serving suggestion: Serve as a main course with chapattis and rice.

MUTHIAS

This is a type of stew made in heaven! Try this recipe and you'll never look back.

cooking time: 1 hour 30 minutes   *serves:* 6

For the dumplings:
150g (5 oz) millet flour
2 tsp crushed garlic
2 tsp grated ginger
1 level tsp salt
¼ tsp chilli powder
2 tbsp desiccated coconut
¼ tsp garam masala
1 handful chopped fenugreek leaves
pinch of turmeric powder
juice of ½ a lemon
1 tbsp oil
125ml (¼ pt) water (and more if required)
For the stew:
4 tbsp oil
2 × 2.5cm (1 inch) cinnamon sticks
3 cardamom pods
7 black peppercorns
6 cloves
2 large onions, finely sliced
3 handfuls of fresh fenugreek leaves, chopped
4 tsp crushed garlic
4 tsp grated ginger
2 tbsp tomato purée
450g (1 lb) peeled, chopped tomatoes
3 tsp coriander powder
1–2 tsp chilli powder
½ tsp turmeric powder
500g (1 lb 2 oz) small pieces of lamb, beef or chicken
200g (7 oz) peas
1 medium aubergine, cut into small pieces
1 large bunch spinach, chopped
2 saragvo singh, cut into 8cm (3 inch) pieces

3 handfuls of fresh coriander leaves, chopped
200g (7 oz) Indian beans (goovar), halved
150g (5 oz) coconut cream
salt to taste
375ml (¾ pt) water
4 medium sized potatoes, peeled and cut into halves

1. Mix together the dumpling ingredients and bind into a dough with the oil and water. Shape into small sausage type dumplings.
2. *For the stew:* Heat the oil, add the whole spices and fry with the onions until golden brown.
3. Add the fenugreek leaves, garlic and ginger.
4. Add tomato purée and allow to cook for at least 1 minute.
5. Then add all the other ingredients EXCEPT for the potatoes and dumplings.
6. When the vegetables are half cooked (about 20 minutes), add the potatoes and dumplings.
7. Allow to boil and then turn the heat to low, cover and simmer for 1 hour.
8. Stir occasionally, and add extra water if necessary.

Serving suggestions: Serve hot as a main course with chapattis and rice or on its own.

BEEF KALIO

An excellent combination of flavours makes this a very rich dish!

cooking time: 1 hour 40 minutes   *serves:* 4–6

oil for deep frying
2 large onions, sliced
4 medium sized potatoes, quartered
800g (1 lb 12 oz) beef cubes
3 tsp crushed garlic
3 tsp grated ginger
4 green chillies, finely sliced
250g (9 oz) peeled, chopped tomatoes
2 tbsp tomato purée
1 tsp garam masala
½ tsp turmeric powder
½ tsp chilli powder
3 tsp coriander powder
1 small carton plain yoghurt (150g)
pinch of saffron
6 cloves
6 black peppercorns
4 cardamom pods, opened
2.5cm (1 inch) cinnamon stick
handful of coriander leaves, chopped
salt to taste

1. Deep fry the onions and potatoes until golden brown (the potatoes do not need to be fully cooked at this stage).
2. Remove the onions and potatoes and set the oil aside. (You can use it to make a Sak.)
3. Put all the ingredients into a large saucepan (including the onions and potatoes), mix, cover and allow to simmer on a low heat for 1 hour, until the beef is tender.

N.B. Wash hands thoroughly after handling chillies.

Serving suggestion: Serve as a main course, with chapattis or naan bread and Spiced Rice.

TANDOORI BEEF SAK

A rich tandoori flavoured curry eaten as the main course.

cooking time: 1 hour   *serves:* 4–6
                     + marinading time

800g (1 lb 12 oz) beef
1 small carton of plain yoghurt (150g)
4 tsp crushed garlic
4 tsp grated ginger
5 tbsp Tandoori powder
1 tsp chilli powder
1 tbsp oil
250g (9 oz) peeled, chopped tomatoes
1 tbsp tomato purée
2 tsp coriander powder
salt to taste
oil for frying
1 large onion, sliced

1. Marinade the beef in a mixture of all of the above ingredients, EXCEPT for the oil and onion, for at least 2 hours, preferably overnight.
2. Heat the oil and fry the onion until dark brown, looking as though it were almost burnt and add to the marinade mixture in a large saucepan.
3. Cover and simmer for 1 hour, until the meat is tender.

Serving suggestion: Serve with naan bread and Spiced Rice.

KEBAB SAK

This is a type of meatball curry, made with fried kebabs in a delicious sauce.

cooking time: 1 hour 50 minutes   *serves:* 4–6

Refer to page 29 for the recipe for the kebabs
For the sauce:
2 tbsp oil
5 cloves
5 black peppercorns
3 cardamom pods, opened
2.5cm (1 inch) cinnamon stick
1 large onion, sliced
3 tsp crushed garlic
2 tsp grated ginger
1 tbsp tomato purée
150g (5 oz) peeled, chopped tomatoes
125ml (¼ pt) water (and more if required)
salt to taste
handful chopped coriander leaves for garnish

1. Follow the recipe on page 29 and make the kebabs.
2. *For the sauce:* Heat the oil and add the whole spices and onion.
3. When the onion has turned golden brown, add the garlic, ginger and tomato purée and fry for 2–3 minutes.
4. Then add the rest of the ingredients (EXCEPT the coriander and the kebabs), stir and cook for 5 minutes.
5. Finally, add about 15 kebabs (DO NOT STIR), cover and simmer for 30 minutes.
6. Garnish with chopped coriander leaves before serving.

Serving suggestion: Serve as a main course with chapattis and rice.

LIVER SAK

An unusual combination of flavours makes this dish distinct. It is a main course dish, although it can be eaten for breakfast too!

cooking time: 50 minutes   *serves:* 4–6

3 tbsp oil
5 cloves
5 black peppercorns
3 cardamom pods, opened
2.5cm (1 inch) cinnamon stick
1 large onion, sliced
250g (9 oz) liver, cut into small pieces
3 tsp crushed garlic
1 tsp grated ginger
1 tbsp tomato purée
150g (5 oz) peeled, chopped tomatoes
¼ tsp turmeric powder
½ tsp chilli powder
3 tsp coriander powder
3 medium sized potatoes, peeled and quartered
125ml (¼ pt) water (and more if required)
salt to taste
handful of chopped coriander leaves for garnish

1. Heat the oil, add the whole spices and onion and fry until the onion is golden brown.
2. Add the liver and fry until brown.
3. Add the garlic and ginger, fry for 1 minute and then add the tomato purée and fry for a further minute.
4. Then add the rest of the ingredients (EXCEPT the chopped coriander), stir, cover and simmer for 40 minutes, until the liver and potatoes have cooked. (While cooking, keep checking to see if more water is required.)
5. Garnish with the chopped coriander leaves before serving.

Serving suggestions: Serve as a main course with Spiced Rice or for breakfast with fried eggs and parathas.

INDIAN CHILLI

This is a hot dish made with minced meat and kidney beans.

cooking time: 1 hour   *serves:* 4

3 tbsp oil
1 large onion, chopped
450g (1 lb) minced beef
2 tsp crushed garlic
2 tsp grated ginger
400g (14 oz) peeled, chopped tomatoes
1 tbsp tomato purée
1 tbsp ground coriander powder
1 tsp chilli powder
2 whole chillies
1 capsicum pepper, chopped
400g (14 oz) kidney beans (see page 11)
250ml (½ pt) water
salt to taste

1. Heat the oil in a saucepan and fry the onion until very lightly brown.
2. Add the minced beef, garlic and ginger and fry until the beef turns brown.
3. Add the rest of the ingredients, bring to the boil, cover and simmer for 50 minutes.

Serving suggestion: Serve with rice and plain yoghurt.

KHEEMA MAYAI

This is a versatile dish, made with minced meat and eggs, eaten either as a main course or for brunch!

cooking time: 1 hour   *serves:* 4

2 tbsp oil
2 cloves
2 black peppercorns
1cm (½ inch) cinnamon stick
1 large onion, sliced
2 tsp crushed garlic
200g (7 oz) mince
1 tbsp tomato purée
115g (4 oz) peeled, chopped tomatoes
2 tsp garam masala
1 tsp coriander powder
½ tsp chilli powder
125ml (¼ pt) water
4 eggs
salt to taste

1. Heat the oil and add the whole spices and onion.
2. When the onion has browned, add the garlic and mince and fry for 10 minutes.
3. Then add the rest of the ingredients (EXCEPT the eggs), stir, cover and simmer for 20 minutes.
4. Transfer into an ovenproof dish and crack the eggs onto the mixture. Cook in a pre-heated oven (190°C, 375°F or gas mark 5) for a further 30 minutes, until the eggs have cooked.

Serving suggestion: Serve hot with parathas.

MAYAI SAK
Plain and simple egg curry.

cooking time: 50 minutes   *serves:* 6

2 tbsp oil
4 cloves
4 cardamom pods, opened
2.5cm (1 inch) cinnamon stick
4 black peppercorns
1 medium sized onion, sliced
2 tsp crushed garlic
2 tbsp tomato purée
150g (5 oz) peeled, chopped tomatoes
2 tsp coriander powder
¼ tsp turmeric powder
½ tsp chilli powder
6 hard boiled eggs
4 medium sized potatoes, peeled and quartered
salt to taste
handful of chopped coriander leaves for garnish

1. Heat the oil and add the whole spices and onion.
2. When the onion has browned, add the garlic and tomato purée and fry for 2 minutes.
3. Then add the rest of the ingredients (EXCEPT for the coriander leaves), stir, cover and simmer for 40 minutes.
4. Garnish with chopped coriander leaves before serving.

Serving suggestion: Serve as a main course with chapattis and rice.

SCRAMBLED EGGS
A very simple, tasty, quick and easy-to-make dish.

cooking time: 20 minutes   *serves:* 4

½ tbsp oil
1 small onion, sliced
1 tsp black mustard seeds
6 eggs, whisked
¼ tsp turmeric powder
¼ tsp salt
¼ tsp chilli powder

1. Heat the oil and fry the onion, until soft.
2. Add the mustard seeds and when they start to pop add the rest of the ingredients and stir vigorously until the eggs have scrambled.

N.B. Make sure the heat is on low when adding mustard seeds, as they are likely to pop.

Serving suggestions: Serve with naan bread as a quick snack or for breakfast with parathas or puris.

VEGETABLES

VEGETABLE SAK

A vegetarian's delight of a very simple sauce transforming vegetables into a main course, e.g. cauliflower or aubergines and potatoes; chick peas; courgettes; mixed vegetables; or any other combination you care to choose!

cooking time: 30 minutes   *serves:* 4–6

2 tbsp oil
1 tsp black mustard seeds
3 tsp crushed garlic
1 tsp grated ginger
1 tbsp tomato purée
150g (5 oz) peeled, chopped tomatoes
2 tsp coriander powder
¼ tsp turmeric powder
½ tsp chilli powder
500g (1 lb 2 oz) vegetables of your choice, chopped
salt to taste
125ml (¼ pt) water
coriander leaves for garnish

1. Heat the oil, turn heat to low and add mustard seeds.
2. When the mustard seeds start to pop, add the garlic and ginger and stir for 2 minutes.
3. Add the tomato purée and cook for 1 minute, before adding the rest of the ingredients (EXCEPT for the water and coriander leaves). Stir together.
4. Add the water, cover and simmer on low heat for 25–30 minutes, until the vegetables have cooked. (It may be necessary to add more water while cooking the vegetables.)
5. Garnish with chopped coriander leaves before serving.

N.B. Make sure the heat is on low when adding mustard seeds, as they are likely to pop.

Serving suggestions: Serve as a main course with chapattis, parathas, puris and/or rice.

KARELA SAK

This is quite a strong flavoured vegetable curry which is normally made in small quantities as a dry dish to be accompanied with wet dishes like Daal.

cooking time: 40 minutes   *serves:* 4

2 karelas
2 tbsp oil
1 large onion, finely sliced
1 tsp crushed garlic
1 tsp grated ginger
2 tsp tomato purée
85g (3 oz) peeled, chopped tomatoes
1 tsp coriander powder
¼ tsp turmeric powder
chilli powder to taste
salt to taste
water, as required

1. Core the karelas, discard the seeds and slice into fine rings.
2. Heat the oil and fry the karela rings until lightly brown.
3. Next, add the onion and fry until soft and, again, just lightly brown.
4. Add the garlic and ginger, stir and allow to fry for 1 minute.
5. Then add the tomato purée and let it stand in the oil for at least 1 minute before stirring.
6. Finally, add the rest of the ingredients and stir.
7. If the mixture is too dry add a small drop of water then cover and cook on a low heat for at least ½ hour, stirring frequently.

Serving suggestion: Serve as a main course with Daal, chapattis and rice, accompanied with some plain yoghurt.

CHUGU KASORI

This dish has a very nutty flavour yet the taste of the corn still comes through. It is an unusual but delicious combination of flavours.

cooking time: 1 hour   *serves:* 4–6

300g (11 oz) fresh peanuts
250ml (½ pt) water
2 tbsp oil
1 tsp black mustard seeds
3 tsp crushed garlic
1 tsp grated ginger
2 tbsp tomato purée
150g (5 oz) peeled, chopped tomatoes
600g (1 lb 4 oz) sweetcorn
**   OR 3 sweetcorn cobs cut into 3 pieces each**
1 tsp chilli powder (or to taste)
¼ tsp turmeric powder
2 tsp coriander powder
2 whole green chillies (optional)
salt to taste
fresh coriander leaves, chopped for garnish

1. Liquidise the peanuts into a coarse mixture with 125ml (¼ pt) of the water.
2. Heat the oil in a saucepan and carefully add the mustard seeds.
3. When the seeds start popping, add the garlic and ginger and stir.
4. Add the tomato purée and chopped tomatoes and allow to cook for 2 minutes.
5. Add the rest of the ingredients (EXCEPT the coriander leaves) and stir.
6. Add the remaining 125ml (¼ pt) water, bring to the boil, lower the heat, cover and simmer for 40 minutes. (It may be necessary to add more water during cooking.)
7. Garnish with chopped coriander leaves before serving.

Note: You can use 3 tbsp peanut butter instead of the liquidised raw peanuts and water.

N.B. Make sure the heat is on low when adding mustard seeds, as they are likely to pop.
Wash hands thoroughly after handling chillies.

Serving suggestion: Serve with chapattis and rice.

KIDNEY BEAN SAK
A very healthy, delicious tasting dish.

cooking time: 40 minutes　　　　　　　　　　　　*serves:* 4

2 tbsp oil
2.5cm (1 inch) cinnamon stick
5 cloves
3 black peppercorns
1 medium sized onion, sliced
2 tsp crushed garlic
1 tbsp tomato purée
150g (5 oz) peeled, chopped tomatoes
2 tsp coriander powder
¼ tsp turmeric powder
½ tsp chilli powder (or to taste)
400g (14 oz) can kidney beans, drained
125–250ml (¼–½ pt) water
salt to taste
handful of coriander leaves, chopped, for garnish

1. Heat the oil and add the whole spices and onion, and fry until the onion is light golden brown.
2. Add the garlic and tomato purée and fry for 2 minutes.
3. Then add the rest of the ingredients (EXCEPT for the coriander leaves), cover and simmer for 30 minutes.
4. Garnish with the chopped coriander leaves before serving.

Serving suggestion: Serve as a main course with chapattis and rice.

URAD

This is a black lentil with its own exceptional taste and this dish does it justice!

cooking time: 1 hour 30 minutes   *serves:* 4–6
        + pre-soaking time

230g (8 oz) urad, soaked overnight
For boiling the urad:
500ml (1 pt) water
½ onion, sliced
2 cloves
2.5cm (1 inch) cinnamon stick
1 tsp salt
For the sauce:
3 tbsp oil
3 cloves
3 black peppercorns
2.5cm (1 inch) cinnamon stick
1 large onion, sliced
3 tsp crushed garlic
1 tsp grated ginger
2 tsp tomato purée
150g (5 oz) peeled, chopped tomatoes
¼ tsp turmeric powder
3 tsp coriander powder
½ tsp chilli powder (or to taste)
1 tsp salt
210ml (7 oz) plain yoghurt
250ml (½ pt) water
handful of chopped coriander leaves for garnish

1. Soak the urad overnight. Drain.
2. Boil the urad and the other ingredients listed 'for boiling' in a saucepan for 40 minutes and drain.
3. *For the sauce:* Heat the oil in another saucepan, add the whole spices and onion and fry until the onion has browned.
4. Add the garlic and ginger and fry for 2 minutes, stirring frequently.

5. Add the rest of the ingredients (EXCEPT the coriander leaves) and the urad, stir, bring to the boil, cover and simmer for 40 minutes.
6. Garnish with the chopped coriander leaves before serving.

Serving suggestion: Serve as a main course with chapattis, rice and raita as an accompaniment.

POTATO SAK

This is a slightly different flavoured dish from that described under 'Vegetable Sak' – but it is equally delicious!

cooking time: 40 minutes   *serves:* 4–6

2 tbsp oil
1 tsp mustard seeds
2 tsp crushed garlic
2 tsp grated ginger
1 tsp tomato purée
50g (2 oz) peeled, chopped tomatoes
2 tsp coriander powder
¼ tsp turmeric powder
½ tsp chilli powder
handful coriander leaves, chopped
handful fenugreek leaves, chopped
6 medium sized potatoes, peeled and cut into small cubes
125ml (¼ pt) water
salt to taste

1. Heat the oil and add the mustard seeds. When they start to pop add the rest of the ingredients and stir.
2. Cover and simmer for 30 minutes until the potatoes have softened.

N.B. Make sure the heat is on low when adding mustard seeds, as they are likely to pop.

Serving suggestion: Serve hot as a main course with puris or parathas.

MOONG SAK

A healthy dish, rich in fibre and very tasty – just try it!

cooking time: 1 hour 25 minutes   *serves:* 4–6
            + pre-soaking time

150g (5 oz) moong beans, soaked overnight
2 tbsp oil
2.5cm (1 inch) cinnamon stick
3 cloves
1 large onion, sliced
1 tsp black mustard seeds
3 tsp crushed garlic
1 tsp grated ginger
2 tsp tomato purée
200g (7 oz) peeled, chopped tomatoes
1 tsp sugar
2 tsp coriander powder
¼ tsp turmeric powder
½ tsp chilli powder (or to taste)
salt to taste
freshly chopped coriander for garnish

1. Soak the moong beans overnight. Drain.
2. In fresh water, boil the soaked moong beans for 50 minutes, until mushy, and drain.
3. Heat the oil and add the cinnamon, cloves and onion.
4. Fry the onion until lightly brown.
5. Add the mustard seeds, and as they begin to pop add the garlic and ginger.
6. Next, add the tomato purée, tomatoes and the rest of the ingredients (EXCEPT the coriander).
7. Stir in the moong beans and allow to boil, then simmer on a low heat for 30 minutes.
8. Garnish with the coriander and serve.

N.B. Make sure the heat is on low when adding mustard seeds, as they are likely to pop.

Serving suggestion: Serve with chapattis and rice.

BHURTHO

This dish is made with the flesh of an aubergine. It can be eaten as part of a main course or as a dip.

cooking time: 1 hour   *serves:* 4–6

1 large aubergine (MUST BE LARGE)
oil for brushing
2 tbsp oil
1 small onion, finely chopped
2 tsp crushed garlic
2 green chillies, finely chopped
salt to taste
water, if required

1. Brush the aubergine's skin with oil and grill until the skin is nearly burnt and the flesh of the aubergine is soft.
2. Peel the skin off the aubergine and mash the flesh into a pulp.
3. Heat the oil in a saucepan, add the onion and garlic and stir.
4. When the onion has softened, add the rest of the ingredients (EXCEPT the water) and stir.
5. Cover and simmer on low heat for at least 20 minutes and add drops of water if the mixture starts to stick to the pan (there is usually enough moisture in the aubergine pulp to aid the cooking process).
6. Stir frequently during cooking.

N.B. Wash hands thoroughly after handling chillies.

Serving suggestions: Serve as a hot dip or with chapattis, Daal Khichri and plain yoghurt.

BINDA SAK

Binda is the Indian name for okra. This recipe gives an unusual combination of flavours that must be tried!

cooking time: 50 minutes   *serves:* 4–6

300g (11 oz) binda
4 tbsp oil
4 medium sized potatoes, peeled and cut into small cubes
1 tsp mustard seeds
2 tsp crushed garlic
1 tsp tomato purée
50g (2 oz) peeled, chopped tomatoes
¼ tsp turmeric powder
¼ tsp chilli powder
2 tsp coriander powder
salt to taste
water, if required

1. Wipe the binda with a clean, dry cloth, cut the ends off and slice into small rings.
2. Heat the oil and fry the binda rings until golden brown. Transfer to a plate.
3. Fry the cubed potatoes until golden brown and also transfer to a plate.
4. Remove any excess oil, leaving only 1 tbsp in the pan, and add the mustard seeds. When they start popping, add the garlic, tomato purée and tomatoes, stir and cook for 5 minutes.
5. Then add the rest of the ingredients along with the fried binda and potatoes. Add some drops of water if the dish gets too dry.
6. Stir, cover and simmer for 25 minutes.

N.B. Make sure the heat is on low when adding mustard seeds, as they are likely to pop.

Serving suggestion: Serve as a main course, accompanied with Daal, chapattis and rice.

GOOVAR SAK

This is a bean which has a distinct flavour of its own. It is quite a treat!

cooking time: 50 minutes   *serves:* 4–6

3 tbsp oil
3 cloves
3 black peppercorns
2.5cm (1 inch) cinnamon stick
1 medium sized onion, sliced
2 tsp crushed garlic
2 tsp tomato purée
85g (3 oz) peeled, chopped tomatoes
3 tsp coriander powder
¼ tsp turmeric powder
½ tsp chilli powder
1 tsp salt (or to taste)
450g (1 lb) goovar
3 medium sized potatoes, peeled and cut into small cubes
125ml (¼ pt) water

1. Heat the oil and add the whole spices and onion and fry until the onion has browned.
2. Add the garlic and tomato purée and fry for 2 minutes, stirring frequently.
3. Add the rest of the ingredients, stir, cover and simmer for 40 minutes until the goovar is tender to touch.

N.B. To prepare the goovar, nip the ends, break in half and then rinse in water.
This dish can be altered slightly by adding some aubergines or peas.

Serving suggestion: Serve as a main course, with Daal as an accompaniment, chapattis and rice.

DAAL

This is a lentil soup, served either on its own, as a soup, or as a sauce with a dry sak.

cooking time: 40 minutes   *serves:* 4
                    + pre-soaking time

85g (3 oz) lentils, washed and soaked for at least
  30 minutes
1 tbsp oil
1 tsp black mustard seeds
3 cloves
4 black peppercorns
2–3 curry leaves
150g (5 oz) peeled, chopped tomatoes
1 tsp crushed garlic
¼ tsp sugar
1 whole green chilli
⅛ tsp turmeric powder
¼ tsp red chilli powder
salt to taste
water as required
handful of finely chopped coriander for garnish

1. Wash and soak the lentils for at least ½ hour or overnight for best results. Drain.
2. Heat the oil in a saucepan and turn the heat to low.
3. Add the mustard seeds, cloves, peppercorns and curry leaves.
4. When the mustard seeds start to pop, add the lentils and the rest of the ingredients (EXCEPT the coriander), adding water according to the 'soup' consistency you require.
5. Bring to the boil, lower the heat, cover and simmer for at least 40 minutes, until the lentils are mushy.
6. Liquidise or whisk the soup and garnish with coriander before serving.

N.B. Wash hands thoroughly after handling chillies.
Mustard seeds may pop, so keep the heat on low and take

care when cooking them.

Serving suggestions: Serve as a soup or as a side dish with a dry vegetable or fish sak, chapattis and rice.

BHAJI
A healthy, delicious dish made with spinach that goes well with the Khichris.

cooking time: 40 minutes   *serves:* 4–6

2–4 large bunches of spinach
3 tbsp oil
4 tsp crushed garlic
150g (5 oz) peeled, chopped tomatoes
½ tsp chilli powder
**   OR 3 finely chopped green chillies (see page 9)**
salt to taste
water, if required

1. Clean and finely chop the spinach*.
2. Heat the oil in a saucepan.
3. Add the garlic and spinach, and then the rest of the ingredients.
4. Stir and add a drop of water if required (not always necessary).
5. Cover and cook on low heat for at least 40 minutes, stirring occasionally.

*Spinach contains enough juices to allow it to cook without needing any extra water. After washing the spinach thoroughly, mop it dry with kitchen paper towels.

Serving suggestion: Serve as a main course with either Moong Bean or Daal Khichri and some plain yoghurt.

6

RICE

RINGRA KHICHRI

An excellent, healthy combination of simple ingredients such as aubergines and moong beans makes up this tasty dish.

cooking time: 50 minutes   *serves:* 4–6

2 tbsp oil
3 cloves
3 black peppercorns
2.5cm (1 inch) cinnamon stick
3 cardamom pods, opened
1 tsp whole cumin seeds
1 small onion, finely sliced
2 tsp crushed garlic
85g (3 oz) peeled, chopped tomatoes
1 small aubergine, cut into 2.5cm (1 inch) cubes
2 medium sized potatoes, peeled and quartered
85g (3 oz) split moong beans
150g (5 oz) rice
250ml (½ pt) water (more if required)
1 tsp salt (or to taste)
50g (2 oz) butter or margarine

1. Heat the oil and add all the whole spices and the onion and fry until the onion has softened.
2. Add the garlic, fry for 2 minutes, and then add the rest of the ingredients, EXCEPT the butter.
3. Stir, cover and simmer for 40 minutes.
4. Keep checking to ensure the mixture is not drying up, and, if necessary, add drops of water to aid the cooking and keep it moist.
5. Ten minutes before serving, add the butter in small blobs.

Serving suggestion: Serve as an accompaniment with a main course of Vegetable Sak.

MEAT PILAU
Savoury rice, great as a main meal or even for a buffet.

cooking time: 1 hour 20 minutes   *serves:* 4–6
                  + pre-soaking time

450g (1 lb) rice, washed and soaked for 40 minutes
500g (1 lb 2 oz) lamb, beef or chicken pieces
250ml (½ pt) water
4 tsp crushed garlic
4 tsp grated ginger
4 green chillies, whole or chopped
3 tbsp oil
1 large onion, sliced
2 tsp cumin seeds
3 cardamom pods
2 × 2.5cm (1 inch) sticks cinnamon
8 cloves
8 black peppercorns
handful of chopped coriander leaves
150g (5 oz) peeled, chopped tomatoes
6 small potatoes peeled and cut into halves
250ml (½ pt) stock* or water
salt to taste
25g (1 oz) butter or margarine

1. Wash and soak the rice, then drain it.
2. Put the meat or chicken in a saucepan with the measured quantity of water, add half of the garlic, ginger and chillies and cook for 30 minutes, until tender.
3. Heat the oil in a separate saucepan.
4. Add the onion, cumin seeds, cardamom pods, cinnamon, cloves and peppercorns.
5. When the onion has softened, add the remaining garlic, ginger and chillies and cook for 2 minutes.
6. Next, add the meat or chicken, the coriander, tomatoes, rice and potatoes.
7. If the meat has been pre-cooked (see below*) add the

resulting stock, made up to 250ml (½ pt) with more water if required. If the meat has not been pre-cooked, just add the same quantity of water.

8. Add salt to taste, bring to the boil, cover and simmer on low heat for 40 minutes, until the rice has cooked.

9. Add the butter or margarine in blobs while the pilau is hot.

*The meat could be pre-cooked with a handful of chopped onions mixed with crushed garlic/ginger, a few cloves and peppercorns, cardamom, a small piece of cinnamon, 2 tsp of cumin seeds and 250ml (½ pt) water. The stock is then used to make the sauce instead of just water.

N.B. Always wash hands thoroughly after handling chillies.
To prevent rice going mushy, never stir while it is cooking.

Serving suggestion: Serve as a main course with 'Mum's' Salad, raita and pickles.

PEAS & POTATO PILAU

Savoury rice made with very simple ingredients.

cooking time: 1 hour 20 minutes   *serves:* 4–6
        + pre-soaking time

450g (1 lb) rice, washed and soaked for 40 minutes
3 tbsp oil
1 large onion, sliced
2 tsp cumin seeds
3 cardamom pods
2 × 2.5cm (1 inch) cinnamon sticks
8 cloves
8 black peppercorns
4 tsp crushed garlic
4 tsp grated ginger
4 green chillies, whole or chopped
handful of chopped coriander leaves
150g (5 oz) peeled, chopped tomatoes
200g (7 oz) peas
6 medium sized potatoes, peeled and quartered
4–6 hard boiled eggs
250ml (½ pt) water
salt to taste
25g (1 oz) butter or margarine

1. Wash and soak the rice, then drain it.
2. Heat the oil in a large saucepan and add the onion,
   cumin seeds, cardamom pods, cinnamon sticks, cloves
   and peppercorns.
3. When the onion has softened, add the garlic, ginger,
   chillies and coriander and cook for 2 minutes.
4. Next, add the tomatoes, peas, potatoes, eggs, water,
   salt and rice and stir.
5. Bring to the boil, cover and simmer on a low heat for
   40 minutes, until the rice has cooked.
6. Add the butter in blobs while the pilau is still hot.

N.B. To prevent rice from going mushy, never stir while it

is cooking.
Wash hands thoroughly after handling chillies.

*Serving suggestion: Serve as a main course with 'Mum's'
Salad, raita and pickles.*

MOONG BEAN KHICHRI

cooking time: 40 minutes   *serves:* 4–6
                    + pre-soaking time

85g (3 oz) split moong beans ⎫ **washed and soaked for**
150g (5 oz) rice   ⎬ **at least 30 minutes**
500ml (1 pt) water
1 tsp salt (or to taste)
50g (2 oz) butter or margarine

1. Wash the grains and soak for at least half an hour.
2. Put all the ingredients in a saucepan EXCEPT for the
    butter.
3. Bring to the boil, cover and simmer for 40 minutes
    until cooked to a very mushy appearance. (It may be
    necessary to add more water during cooking if the
    mixture becomes too dry.)
4. Finally, add the butter and stir in before serving.

Serving suggestion: Serve with a vegetable sak.

SPICED RICE

This is a simple rice dish with just a hint of spice.

cooking time: 45 minutes   *serves:* 4
           + pre-soaking time

**250g (9 oz) basmati or long grain rice, washed and soaked
  for at least 30 minutes**
1 tbsp oil
4 cloves
4 black peppercorns
1 tsp cumin seeds
2.5cm (1 inch) cinnamon stick
3 cardamom pods, opened
1 very small onion, sliced
250ml (½ pt) water
2 tsp salt

1. Wash and soak the rice. Drain.
2. Heat the oil and add all the spices and onion.
3. When the onion is soft, add the rice.
4. Add the water and salt, stir and bring to the boil.
5. Lower the heat, cover and simmer for 40 minutes until
   the rice is soft to touch.

N.B. To prevent the rice from going mushy, do not stir
during cooking.

Serving suggestion: Serve with any of the saks.

CHINESE-STYLE RICE

A very simple dish that will utilise leftovers and, although not Indian, is nice in combination with some of the dry dishes!

cooking time: 50 minutes   *serves:* 4–6
                      + pre-soaking time

400g (14 oz) rice, washed and soaked for 30 minutes
salt to taste
150g (5 oz) mixed vegetables (diced carrots, green peppers,
    beans, etc.)
1 large onion, sliced
3 tsp crushed garlic
5 tsp grated ginger
2 tbsp oil
50g (2 oz) prawns (optional)
50g (2 oz) cooked chicken bits (optional)
2 eggs
1 tsp tabasco sauce (or to taste)
3 tbsp soy sauce
ground black pepper to taste

1. Wash, soak and drain the rice, then boil it in fresh water, adding salt to taste, until just cooked (about 40 minutes). Drain and rinse.
2. Stir fry the vegetables with the onion, garlic and ginger and put aside.
3. Stir fry the prawns and chicken bits (if using) and put aside.
4. Scramble the eggs and put aside.
5. Put all the ingredients EXCEPT the rice, eggs and black pepper into the fry-pan, stir and heat gently.
6. Carefully mix all the ingredients into the rice and serve.

Serving suggestions: Serve on its own or with Tandoori Chicken.

MEAT BIRYANI

This is an absolutely delicious dish of beef in a rich sauce between layers of rice. It's easy to make, too!

cooking time: 2 hours   *serves:* 4–6
+ pre-soaking time

675g (1½ lb) rice, washed and soaked for 40 minutes
For the sauce:
oil for deep frying
2 large onions, sliced
4 medium sized potatoes, quartered
675g (1½ lb) beef, cubed
3 tsp crushed garlic
3 tsp grated ginger
4 green chillies, finely sliced
250g (9 oz) peeled, chopped tomatoes
2 tbsp tomato purée
1 tsp garam masala
½ tsp turmeric powder
½ tsp chilli powder
3 tsp coriander powder
1 small carton plain yoghurt (150g)
pinch of saffron
6 cloves
6 black peppercorns
4 cardamom pods, opened
2.5cm (1 inch) cinnamon stick
handful of coriander leaves, chopped
3 hard boiled eggs (optional)
salt to taste
For the rice:
1 ltr (2 pts) or more of water, to cook the rice
1 tbsp salt (or to taste)
For the topping:
2 tbsp oil
4 cloves
4 black peppercorns

(*continued overleaf*)

(*Meat Biryani continued*)
4 cardamom pods, opened
2.5cm (1 inch) cinnamon stick
1 tsp whole cumin seeds
1 tbsp yellow food colouring

1. *To make the sauce:* Deep fry the onions and potatoes, separately, until golden brown (the potatoes do not need to be fully cooked at this stage). Set the oil aside.
2. Mix all the ingredients (EXCEPT a handful of onions, to be used later) in a large saucepan, cover and simmer on a low heat for 1 hour, until the beef is tender.
3. *For the rice:* Boil the washed, soaked and drained rice for 25 minutes until just cooked (i.e. not mushy) and drain.
4. Take a big ovenproof dish and make alternate layers with the sauce, the rice, the sauce and finally the rice as the top layer.
5. *For the topping:* Heat the oil and add all the ingredients EXCEPT for the food colouring.
6. When the cumin seeds start to fry, remove from the heat and spread over the top layer of rice.
7. Sprinkle the top with the remaining fried onions (saved from earlier) and pour the yellow food colouring over the rice in the shape of a cross.
8. Cover and place in a pre-heated oven (160°C, 325°F or gas mark 3) for 50 minutes, until the biryani has heated through.

N.B. To prevent rice from going mushy, never stir while it is cooking.
Wash hands thoroughly after handling chillies.
The layers should be kept distinct when serving up this dish.

Serving suggestion: Serve as a main course, with plain yoghurt and pickles of your choice.

DAAL KHICHRI
Another type of khichri made with a mixture of rice and lentils.

cooking time: 50 minutes   *serves:* 4
             + pre-soaking time

150g (5 oz) rice } washed and soaked for
85g (3 oz) daal } at least 30 minutes
1 tbsp oil
5 cloves
5 black peppercorns
2.5cm (1 inch) cinnamon stick
1 tsp jeera seeds
1 very small onion, finely sliced
250ml (½ pt) water
½ tsp turmeric powder
2 tsp salt (or to taste)

1. Wash and soak the grains.
2. Heat the oil, add the whole spices and the onion, and cook until onion softens.
3. Add the grains, the water, the turmeric and salt.
4. Bring to the boil, cover and simmer on low heat for 40 minutes until grains are soft to the touch.

N.B. Do not stir this dish when cooking or it will go mushy!

Serving suggestions: Serve with Potato Sak, Vegetable Sak or Bhaji.

7

BREADS

NAAN BREAD

This is made with very simple, healthy ingredients and is delicious when freshly made! You can be ambitious and experiment by adding other ingredients such as garlic, very finely chopped onion, whole cumin seeds, etc.

cooking time: 1 hour 30 minutes   *serves:* 4–6

450g (1 lb) plain flour
1 tsp sugar
½ tsp salt
½ tsp bicarbonate of soda
1 tsp baking powder
2 tbsp dried yeast
2–3 tbsp plain yoghurt
1 egg
125ml (¼ pt) milk
50g (2 oz) butter or margarine

1. Mix all the dry ingredients with the yeast, yoghurt and egg.
2. Warm the milk and add to the dry mixture a little at a time until the dough forms. (It is possible that not all of the milk will be required: the dough should be firm and not soggy.)
3. Turn the dough onto a floured surface and knead for at least 5 minutes.
4. Put in a lightly floured bowl, cover with a wet cloth and leave in a warm place to rise for at least 40 minutes or until the dough has doubled in size and springs back easily when lightly pressed.
5. Return dough to a floured surface and knead again. Divide into 6 or 8 equal size balls and allow to rise for about 20 minutes in a warm place until they have almost doubled in size and spring back easily when pressed.
6. Roll out the balls with a rolling pin on a floured surface or flatten in the palms of your hands to about ½cm (¼ inch) thick.

7. Brush with melted butter and cook under a hot grill until golden brown, and repeat on the other side.

N.B. The grill should not be too hot to ensure that the naan is allowed to cook before it turns golden brown.

Serving suggestions: Serve with any of the saks or stuffed with Kebabs, finely sliced cabbage, onion, cucumber and a squeeze of lemon juice.

CHAPATTIS

cooking time: 50 minutes   *serves:* 4–6

450g (1 lb) chapatti flour
2 tbsp oil
¼ tsp salt
hot water

1. Mix together the flour, oil and salt and add just enough hot water to bind into a dough.
2. Take walnut size pieces of the dough and roll each one into a ball in the palms of your hands for 1 minute.
3. Next, roll out each ball into a very thin flat circle with a thin rolling pin.
4. Heat a fry-pan and dry cook both sides (i.e. without any oil) until just brown.

Serving suggestion: Serve with saks.

SPICY PARATHAS

An excellent type of chapatti, with a combination of flavours.

cooking time: 1 hour   *serves:* 6

450g (1 lb) chapatti flour
¼ tsp salt
3 tbsp oil
¼ tsp turmeric powder
¼ tsp chilli powder
handful of chopped coriander and fenugreek leaves
hot water
oil for frying

1. Mix together all the ingredients (EXCEPT for the frying oil), adding just enough hot water to bind into a dough.
2. Heat a frying pan and turn the heat down to medium.
3. Divide the dough into six equal sized balls and roll each one in the palms of your hands for 1 minute.
4. Roll out into thickened chapatti shapes.
5. **Without any oil,** part cook both sides in the frying pan until just brown.
6. Next, fry both sides with a drop of oil until golden.

Serving suggestions: Serve hot with saks, pickles or for breakfast with fried eggs, jam or anything that takes your fancy!

PLAIN PARATHAS

Very similar to the above but without the spices, these have their own distinctive taste. Follow the method above.

450g (1 lb) chapatti flour
¼ tsp salt
3 tbsp oil
hot water
oil for frying

PURIS

These again are a type of chapatti but are much smaller, deep fried and different in taste. These will keep for several days in an air tight container.

cooking time: 50 minutes   *serves:* 6

200g (7 oz) plain flour
200g (7 oz) chapatti flour
3 tbsp oil
¼ tsp salt
¼ tsp turmeric powder
hot water
oil for deep frying

1. Mix together all the ingredients (EXCEPT the oil for frying), adding just enough hot water to bind into a dough.
2. Heat the oil for frying.
3. Divide the dough into equal sized balls, the size of walnuts.
4. Roll out into small, thin chapatti shapes.
5. Immerse in the hot oil and deep fry, until both sides are golden brown.

Serving suggestions: Serve with Kheer or for breakfast with fried eggs or murbo.

8

SWEETS

CARROT & APRICOT 'PUD'
An excellent combination of flavours – must be tried!

cooking time: 1 hour   *serves:* 6
                    + setting time

50g (2 oz) dried apricots
½ tbsp custard powder
375ml (¾ pt) milk
dash of rum, cognac or sherry (optional)
600g (1 lb 4 oz) carrots, finely grated
25g (1 oz) cashew nuts, chopped into small pieces
25g (1 oz) pistachio nuts, chopped into small pieces
150g (5 oz) sweetened condensed milk
115g (4 oz) evaporated milk
For decoration:
1 large carton double cream, whipped (234ml/14 oz)
grated chocolate or desiccated coconut
almonds, coarsely chopped
cherries or kiwi fruit slices

1. Soak apricots until soft (about 10 minutes) and cut into small pieces.
2. Mix the custard powder into a smooth paste with a small amount of milk.
3. Boil the rest of the milk (adding the alcohol, if using).
4. Add the carrots, stir and allow to cook for 5 minutes.
5. Stir in the cashew and pistachio nuts along with the custard paste, followed by the condensed and evaporated milks. Mix well.
6. Pour into a bowl and when cool put into the fridge to set.
7. Spread the double cream over and decorate.

Serving suggestion: Serve scoops in a shallow fruit bowl.

MILK SEV

A milk 'pud' made with vermicelli and spices.

cooking time: 1 hour   *serves:* 4–6

115g (4 oz) butter
4 cardamom pods, opened
2.5cm (1 inch) cinnamon stick
150g (5 oz) vermicelli
115g (4 oz) sultanas
1 tsp ground nutmeg
1 tsp ground cinnamon
750ml (1½ pt) milk
2 strands saffron
50g (2 oz) coarsely chopped almonds
50g (2 oz) coarsely chopped pistachio nuts

1. Melt the butter on a low heat, add the whole spices and fry for 5 minutes.
2. Scrunch the vermicelli and add to the butter. Fry for 10 minutes until golden brown, stirring constantly.
3. Add the sultanas and fry for 5 minutes, still stirring frequently.
4. Add the rest of the ingredients and bring to the boil.
5. Cover and simmer for 40 minutes, until the vermicelli is tender to touch.

Serving suggestion: Serve hot as it is!

KULFI

A type of rich ice-cream, fit for a king! So, if you are up to it, have a try!

cooking time: 40 minutes   *serves:* 6
              + freezing time

2 medium sized eggs
200g (7 oz) sugar (or to taste)
200g (7 oz) evaporated milk
½ tsp ground cardamom seeds
½ tsp ground nutmeg
½ tsp vanilla essence
2 strands saffron (optional)
50g (2 oz) coarsely chopped almonds
50g (2 oz) coarsely chopped pistachio nuts
250ml (½ pt) double cream, whipped

1. Separate the egg yolks from the whites.
2. Whisk the sugar, milk, cardamom seeds and nutmeg until frothy.
3. Add the vanilla essence and saffron, if using, to the egg yolks, beat and add to the milk mixture.
4. Whisk the egg whites until firm and add to the mixture.
5. Add the nuts and cream and mix very gently.
6. Freeze for ½–1 hour.
7. Remove from freezer, stir and place into moulds and re-freeze for 1–2 hours.
8. Allow to thaw for 10 minutes before serving.

Serving suggestion: Serve decorated with cherries, ground almonds or chocolate sauce.

FRUIT SALAD

This is an absolutely delicious fruit salad, right for any occasion!

preparation time: 40 minutes   *serves:* 6
                    + chilling time

**150g (5 oz) mixed tropical fruit in fruit juice (ready
    bought)**
2 passion fruits, halve, scoop out flesh and discard skin
1 pomegranate, peel and use ONLY the seeds (flesh is bitter)
1 banana, sliced
1 hard pear, peeled and cubed
handful of seedless grapes, halved
2 kiwi fruits, peeled and sliced
1 small red apple, cubed
½ ripe mango, peeled and cubed
½ pawpaw, peeled, seeded and cut into chunks
6 lychees, peeled and seeded
½ star fruit, thinly sliced
2 tbsp sugar (optional)
1 tbsp alcohol of your choice (optional)

Mix all the ingredients together and chill for at least 1 hour before serving.

Serving suggestions: Serve plain or with ice-cream or single cream.

GULAB JAMBOOS

These are for the very sweet toothed – guaranteed to make you even sweeter!

cooking time: 1 hour   *serves:* 6
+ standing time

For the jamboos:
250g (9 oz) gulab jamboo powder
250g (9 oz) semolina
1 tsp sugar
1 tsp ground cardamom seeds
1 level tsp baking powder
pinch of bicarbonate of soda
2 tbsp oil
oil for frying
125–250ml (¼–½ pt) milk
desiccated coconut
For the syrup:
300g (11 oz) sugar
250ml (½ pt) water
For decoration:
chopped almonds (optional)

1. *For the jamboos:* Mix together all the ingredients in a bowl EXCEPT for both amounts of oil, the milk and the coconut.
2. Heat the 2 tbsp oil and add.
3. Warm the milk and add a little at a time to bind the mixture into a dough. (You may not need it all.)
4. Roll the dough into small balls the size of walnuts. (You should get about 20 from this quantity of dough.)
5. Heat the oil and deep fry the balls until golden brown and drain on kitchen paper towels. Roll in the desiccated coconut and put into a dish.
6. *For the syrup:* Put the water and sugar in a saucepan, stir and allow to boil until a syrup forms; the liquid will reduce almost to half. (Be careful not to splash yourself as melted sugar is *very* hot.)

7. Pour the syrup over the jamboos and allow to soak for at least 1 hour before serving, decorated with chopped almonds.

N.B. The syrup can be flavoured with grated orange or lemon rind.

Serving suggestion: Serve 3 jamboos with the syrup in a shallow fruit bowl garnished with chopped nuts.

SWEET POTATO PUDDING
This is made with sweet potatoes and milk.

cooking time: 40 minutes *serves:* 4–6
+ chilling time

2–3 sweet potatoes, *not* **peeled**
water for cooking potatoes
375ml (¾ pt) milk
1 small carton single cream (210ml/7 oz) (optional)
sugar to taste
coarsely ground almonds for garnish

1. Place the sweet potatoes in boiling water, cover partly and cook on medium heat for 30 minutes, until the potatoes are easily squashed.
2. Peel the skin off the potatoes and mash into a purée.
3. Mix the potato purée with the milk and cream (if using), and sugar to taste.
4. Chill for at least 2 hours before serving, garnished with the nuts.

Serving suggestion: This pudding is especially nice eaten cold on a hot summer's day. It will follow nicely after any of the main courses in this book.

KERI' N RUUSS

Mango pulp flavoured with ginger, eaten as a cold soup.

preparation time: 2 minutes   *serves:* 6
           + chilling time

1 tbsp ginger powder
1 small carton single cream (210ml/7 oz)
1 large tin mango pulp (450g/1 lb)
2 tbsp granulated sugar

Mix the ginger with a little of the cream into a paste and then mix with all the ingredients (including the remaining cream), stir and chill for at least 1 hour before serving.

Serving suggestion: Serve chilled.

LEMON
AND
GREEN CHILLI
PICKLE

CARROT
PICKLE

9

PICKLES &
ACCOMPANIMENTS

AMBLI

A very tangy chutney made with tamarind, delicious with most foods!

cooking time: 15 minutes   *serves:* 4

100g (3½ oz) dry tamarind
a few dates
   OR 2 tsp sugar } **(optional)**
1 tsp red chilli powder (optional)
500ml (1 pt) water
2 green chillies, finely chopped
coriander leaves, finely chopped for garnish

1. Boil all the ingredients (EXCEPT the green chillies and coriander) in the water.
2. When the water has thickened and reduced in quantity, remove from the heat.
3. Strain through a sieve.
4. Add the green chillies and coriander and allow to cool.

Serving suggestion: Serve as a dip with bhajias, samosas or kebabs.

RAITA

A common yoghurt dish which is easy to make and very refreshing to eat.

preparation time: 15 minutes   *serves:* 4

1 small carton plain yoghurt (150g)
½ tsp cumin seeds, coarsely ground (optional)
¼ cucumber, coarsely grated
2 green chillies, finely chopped (optional)
½ handful of fresh mint, finely chopped
   OR 2 tsp mint sauce
coriander leaves, finely chopped, for garnish

1. Mix all the ingredients (EXCEPT the coriander) into a smooth paste.
2. Garnish with the coriander leaves before serving.

N.B. Wash hands thoroughly after handling chillies.

Serving suggestions: Serve as an accompaniment with any of the main meals or as a dip for bhajias, samosas or kebabs.

FOODINO CHUTNEY
A chutney made with fresh mint and chillies.

preparation time: 10 minutes   *serves:* 4–6

handful of fresh mint leaves
5 green chillies
3 cloves of garlic, peeled
1 tbsp lemon juice
¼ tsp salt

Liquidise all the ingredients together and serve!

N.B. Wash hands thoroughly after handling chillies.

Serving suggestion: Excellent with bhajias.

'MUM'S' SALAD

A special salad as made by my mother, using fresh ingredients and dressed with a hint of malt vinegar!

preparation time: 30 minutes   *serves:* 4
                    + chilling time

1 large carrot, quartered lengthwise and finely sliced
1 large onion, very finely sliced
200g (7 oz) white cabbage, finely shredded
¼ cucumber, cut into small cubes
4 red or white radish, cut into small cubes
3 green chillies, very finely chopped
4 tbsp malt vinegar
salt to taste

Mix all the ingredients together and leave covered in the fridge for at least 40 minutes before serving.

N.B. Wash hands thoroughly after handling chillies.

Serving suggestions: Serve with Peas & Potato Pilau or Meat Pilau, or as an accompaniment with any main course.

SAMBHARO

A quick and easy but delicious pickle made with very simple ingredients.

cooking time: 25 minutes   *serves:* 4–6

2 tbsp oil
1 tsp black mustard seeds
3 cloves garlic, finely sliced
1 large carrot, cut into fine strips
5–10 green chillies, cut into strips
1 small unripe mango, cut into fine strips (optional)
¼ cabbage, finely sliced
¼ tsp turmeric powder
2–3 drops lemon juice
salt to taste
water

1. Heat the oil, add the mustard seeds and garlic.
2. When the mustard seeds start popping, add the rest of the ingredients, with just enough water, if required, to prevent the mixture burning. Stir together.
3. Cover and cook on low heat for 20 minutes, stirring frequently.

N.B. Make sure the heat is on low when adding mustard seeds, as they are likely to pop.
Wash hands thoroughly after handling chillies.

Serving suggestions: Can be served hot or cold as an accompaniment with a main meal or parathas.

MURBO

A delicious preserve, either eaten as a jam or as an accompaniment.

cooking time: 1 hour   *serves:* 6

450g (1 lb) unripe green mangoes
250ml (½ pt) water
300g (11 oz) sugar
5 cloves
5 cardamom pods, opened
5 black peppercorns
5cm (2 inch) cinnamon stick

1. Peel the mango and slice or grate coarsely.
2. Boil the water, sugar and whole spices for 15 minutes.
3. Keep stirring until it forms into a syrup (if too thick, add more water).
4. Add the mangoes and allow to boil for at least 5 minutes.
5. Lower the heat, part cover and allow to simmer for 30 minutes, until the mangoes soften.
6. Take off the heat and allow to cool before serving.

N.B. This can be stored in a cool place for several weeks.

Serving suggestions: Serve as an accompaniment with saks or with hot parathas for breakfast.

CARROT PICKLE
A very easy-to-make tasty pickle!

preparation time: 20 minutes   *serves:* 4–6
                    + marinading time

3 large carrots
2 tsp crushed garlic
¼ tsp salt
1 tbsp oil
1 tsp tomato purée
½ tsp chilli powder
5 whole green chillies, sliced lengthwise (optional)

1. Peel the carrots and slice thinly, lengthwise.
2. Mix with the rest of the ingredients and allow to
    marinate for at least 2 hours before serving.

N.B. Wash hands thoroughly after handling chillies.

*Serving suggestion: Serve as an accompaniment with any
of the main courses.*

LEMON & GREEN CHILLI PICKLE
This, again, is easy to make but very tasty!

preparation time: 20 minutes   *serves:* several portions
                    + 2 weeks for maturing

2 lemons, sliced
10 green chillies, slit lengthwise
3 tbsp lemon juice
125ml (¼ pt) water
1 tsp turmeric powder
1 tbsp salt

1. Mix all the ingredients together in a glass bowl. Transfer into a glass jar and seal tight.
2. Stir at least once a day with a wooden spoon for two weeks.
3. After two weeks the lemons will have softened and the pickle is ready to serve.

N.B. Metal bowls and spoons will taint the flavour of this pickle, so be sure to use glass and wood, as recommended.
Wash hands thoroughly after handling chillies.

Serving suggestion: Serve with whatever takes your fancy!

10

SNACKS

NOORI BISCUITS
A type of shortbread-like biscuit.

cooking time: 50 minutes   *serves:* several

150g (5 oz) butter
115g (4 oz) sugar
1 egg
150g (5 oz) plain flour
½ tsp baking powder
1 tsp ground nutmeg
115g (4 oz) ground almonds
115g (4 oz) fine semolina
whole almonds to decorate

1. Cream the butter and sugar until pale.
2. Add the egg and whisk gently.
3. Sieve the flour, baking powder, ground nutmeg, ground almonds and semolina into the mixture and fold gently into a soft dough.
4. Take small balls the size of walnuts and flatten, then decorate with three almonds before placing on a greased baking tray.
5. Cook in a pre-heated oven (180°C, 350°F or gas mark 4) for 20 minutes, until just golden brown.

Serving suggestions: Snack as you please, or serve as an accompaniment with ice-cream.

MANDAZI

An African-style bread snack, deep fried until golden brown and sprinkled with desiccated coconut. Best eaten hot or will keep for weeks in an airtight container.

cooking time: 1 hour 40 minutes   *serves:* 6

450g (1 lb) plain flour
6 tbsp sugar (or to taste)
50g (2 oz) coconut cream, dissolved in a little boiling water
4 tsp cardamom seeds, coarsely ground
1 tsp butter
1 tbsp dried yeast
1 tsp baking powder
oil for deep frying
desiccated coconut

1. Mix all the ingredients (EXCEPT the oil and desiccated coconut) into a dough.
2. Cover and leave in a warm place to rise and double in size either overnight or for at least 40 minutes.
3. Knead the dough and roll out to 1cm (⅓ inch) thick.
4. Heat the oil.
5. Cut the dough into diamonds or shapes of your choice and fry until golden brown.
6. Drain on kitchen paper towels.
7. Sprinkle with desiccated coconut while hot.

Serving suggestions: Serve hot for breakfast or cold as a snack at tea time or in between meals.

THEPLAS

These are a type of doughnut that can be stored for several weeks and eaten as a snack at your leisure!

cooking time: 1 hour   *serves:* several

450g (1 lb) plain flour
115g (4 oz) brown sugar
3 tsp cardamom seeds, coarsely ground
2 tbsp oil
1 tsp baking powder
handful fennel seeds
hot water, as required
oil for frying

1. Mix all the ingredients (EXCEPT the oil for frying) with just enough hot water to bind into a dough.
2. Heat the oil.
3. In the meantime, roll out the dough into a large circle, ½cm (¼ inch) thick, and cut into any shapes that you desire.
4. Deep fry until golden brown and drain on kitchen paper towels.

N.B. Cool before storing.

Serving suggestion: Goes well with a cup of tea.

AFRICAN RICE CAKES
Absolutely delicious – just try them!

cooking time: 1 hour   *serves:* 6
          + soaking and standing time

450g (1 lb) fat grain rice (i.e. pudding rice)
50g (2 oz) coconut cream
250ml (½ pt) boiling water
500ml (1 pt) milk
230g (8 oz) sugar
2 tsp cardamom seeds, coarsely ground
4 tsp dried yeast
1 egg
oil for frying

1. Soak the rice for 2–3 hours.
2. Melt the coconut cream in boiling water.
3. Drain the rice and mix with the coconut cream, milk, sugar, cardamom seeds and yeast, cover and leave overnight.
4. The next day, add the egg and mix together.
5. Heat some oil in a frying pan and shallow fry one tablespoon of the mixture at a time, turning, until both sides are brown.

Serving suggestion: Eat within a few days, as a snack.

KHARI PURIS

A savoury snack that will keep for weeks in an airtight container.

cooking time: 50 minutes   *serves:* several

450g (1 lb) plain flour
125ml (¼ pt) warm oil
115g (4 oz) gram flour
1 tbsp cumin seeds
1 tsp salt
1 tsp black pepper, coarsely ground
cold water for binding
oil for deep frying

1. Mix all the ingredients together (EXCEPT for the frying oil) and bind using just enough water to create a firm dough.
2. Heat the oil for deep frying.
3. Roll out the dough into a very thin, large circle.
4. Cut into triangles, prick with a fork and deep fry until golden brown.
5. Drain on kitchen paper towels.

Serving suggestions: Serve as a snack or with drinks.

DRINKS

CHAI
This is a tea that is made in a simple way but tastes quite different from the 'English brew'!

cooking time: 15 minutes   *serves:* 4–6

500ml (1 pt) milk
250ml (½ pt) water
3–4 tea bags
   OR 1 tbsp loose black tea
sugar to taste

1. Put all the ingredients in a saucepan, bring to the boil and then simmer on a low heat for 15 minutes.
2. Strain before serving.

Serving suggestion: Serve at any time of day, although it is especially nice at breakfast with parathas or puris.

MASALA CHAI

This again is made with very simple ingredients, but the spices give this tea a rich and distinctive flavour.

cooking time: 25 minutes   *serves:* 4–6

500ml (1 pt) milk
250ml (½ pt) water
3–4 tea bags
   OR 1 tbsp loose black tea
1 tsp ginger powder
3 cloves
3 black peppercorns
2.5cm (1 inch) cinnamon stick
2 cardamom pods
sugar to taste

1. Mix all the ingredients in a saucepan, bring to the boil and then simmer on a low heat for 20 minutes.
2. Strain the tea before serving.

Serving suggestion: This is especially warming on a cold winter day or last thing at night.

LASSI

This is a yoghurt drink which is very refreshing.

preparation time: 5 minutes
+ chilling time

serves: 4–6

210ml (7 oz) yoghurt
500ml (1 pt) water
¼ tsp ground black pepper
pinch of salt

1. Mix all the ingredients in a jug and whisk (either with an electric or hand whisk) until it starts to froth.
2. Place in the fridge for at least 1 hour to chill before serving.

Serving suggestion: This drink is especially nice as an accompaniment with the dry vegetable saks.

KADHO

This is a milk drink that is richly flavoured with ingredients such as saffron and nuts.

cooking time: 30 minutes   *serves:* 6

500ml (1 pt) milk
2 tbsp sweetened condensed milk
115g (4 oz) evaporated milk
¼ tsp ground nutmeg
1 tsp ground cardamom seeds
4 strands saffron
handful of almonds and pistachios, coarsely chopped

Mix all the ingredients together in a saucepan, bring to the boil and simmer for 30 minutes.

Serving suggestion: This is normally served on special occasions, and in small amounts, because it is so rich.

KESAR DOODH

Again, this is milk flavoured with saffron but it is not as rich as the Kadho.

cooking time: 15 minutes   *serves:* 6

500ml (1 pt) milk
3 strands saffron
3 cloves
3 black peppercorns
2.5cm (1 inch) cinnamon stick
2 cardamom pods
handful of almonds and pistachios, coarsely chopped
sugar to taste

Mix all the ingredients in a saucepan, bring to the boil and simmer for 12 minutes. Strain off whole spices and serve.

Serving suggestion: Serve as a night time drink.

RAAB

This drink is made from millet flour and spices.

cooking time: 15 minutes   *serves:* 6

25g (1 oz) butter or margarine
2 × 2.5cm (1 inch) cinnamon sticks
4 cloves
4 black peppercorns
2 tbsp millet powder
50g (2 oz) brown sugar
½ tsp powder ginger
500ml (1 pt) water (or more if required)

1. Melt the butter or margarine in a saucepan and fry the whole spices for 2 minutes.
2. Add the millet flour and fry until it turns brown.
3. Next, add the rest of the ingredients and stir continuously until the mixture boils. Lower the heat and simmer for 20 minutes.

Serving suggestion: Serve hot, either in a mug or a soup bowl. It is very comforting when you have a cold!

GLOSSARY

Ambli	Known as *tamarind* in English. Usually dried, it is the fruit of the Tamarind tree.
Binda	Known as *okra* or '*ladies' fingers*' in English. Green in colour and available fresh and tinned. *Recommendations: best used fresh – never wash them, but always wipe clean with a dry cloth.*
Cardamom	Known as *elichi* in Indian. Green or white pods; seeds or powdered. *Recommendation: use white, opened pods for best results.*
Celery seeds	Known as *ajma* in Indian. Can be hot to taste if eaten raw.
Chillies	Known as *mirchi* in Indian. Can be green or red, whole or just seeds. Always wash hands thoroughly after handling chillies because they cause a burning sensation on the skin which can be transferred to other parts of the body by touch. *Recommendation: use fresh green chillies.*
Chilli powder	Also known as cayenne pepper. Very hot powder. Wash hands thoroughly after handling (see above).
Cinnamon	Known as *taj* in Indian. Available in sticks or ground into powder. *Recommendations: use whole and ground for garam masala.*
Cloves	Known as *laving* in Indian. Available whole or ground. *Recommendations: use whole and ground for garam masala.*
Coriander	Known as *dhania* in Indian. The leaves of the coriander plant are available fresh or as a powder.

Recommendation: use fresh for garnish and in powder form for sauces.

Cumin	Known as *jeera* in Indian. Available in seed or powder form. *Recommendation: use both types according to recipe.*
Curry leaves	Known as *limbri* in Indian. They look like bay leaves and are available fresh or dried (although mainly dried).
Daal	Split, shiny lentils. (Daal is also the name of a dish made with lentils. See page 71.)
Fennel seeds	Aniseed type of flavour.
Fenugreek	Known as *methi* in Indian. Fresh or dried leaves and seeds. *Recommendation: use fresh.*
Garam masala	A combination of ground spices. *Recommendation: make your own, following the recipe on page 9.*
Garlic	Known as *lasan* in Indian. Available fresh or can be bought as paste in jars. *Recommendation: use fresh for best flavour.*
Ginger	Known as *adu* in Indian. Available fresh, as a paste in jars, or powdered. *Recommendation: use fresh according to recipe.*
Goovar	Known as *Indian bean* in English. Green in colour, it is flat and pointed at one end.
Gram flour	A flour made from chick peas, described as gram flour on the packaging.
Gulab jamboo flour	A ready-made flour mix to make jamboos and sold under this name.
Indian bean	(See goovar.)

Karela   A green vegetable which looks like a
                      cucumber with lots of bumps, pointed at
                      both ends. It has a bitter taste.

Lapsi   Cracked wheat (bulgar).

Mustard seeds   Known as *rai* in Indian. Can be black or
                      white.
                      Recommendation: use whole black seeds.

Nutmeg   Known as *jaifar* in Indian. Available
                      whole or ground.
                      *Recommendation: best used freshly
                      ground.*

Okra   Known as *binda* in Indian. (See binda.)

Peppercorns   Known as *mari* in Indian. Available white
                      or black, whole or ground.
                      Recommendation: use whole black corns.

Saffron   Known as *kesar* in Indian. Dried stigmas
                      of the crocus flower, they appear red/
                      orange in colour and are very expensive,
                      although keep for years!
                      Recommendation: use sparingly.

Saragvo singh   Known as *drumsticks* in English. Green
                      in colour, long (with ridges running down
                      lengthwise) and pointed at both ends.

Tamarind   Known as *ambli* in Indian. (See ambli.)

Tandoori   A ready-made mix of spices, red in
  powder   colour.

Tikka powder   A ready-made mix of spices, yellow in
                      colour.

Turmeric   Known as *haldi* in Indian. Available as a
                      whole root or yellow powder.
                      Recommendation: use the powder.

Vermicelli   This is a kind of pasta, which is in the
                      form of fine tubes.

INDEX

Page numbers of recipes are given in bold

HANDBOOK OF HERBS

One of the attractions of growing herbs is their undemanding nature. They flourish with minimal attention. A great many grow happily indoors, providing an all-the-year-round supply. The beauty and fragrance of the many different flowers and leaves in an indoor herb garden give great pleasure. Margot McLeod devotes a chapter to each important herb, taking them in alphabetical order for easy reference. Working in some fascinating historical tit-bits, she deals with growing hints, special uses (such as for health, flower arrangements, etc.) and nearly always a splendid recipe or two. Tea and wine from herbs are included, and there is a chapter on spices.

MICROWAVE COOKING PROPERLY EXPLAINED

Now established as the standard work on basic microwave cooking. Discover how your microwave can become a valuable part of your kitchen team, working together with your hob, grill, toaster, kettle and, on occasions, conventional oven. Whether you are a new microwave owner or an experienced user, Annette Yates will help you get the most from *your* microwave.

Uniform with this book

THE CURRY SECRET

The curry book with a difference! Gives the secret of *Indian Restaurant Cooking*: not the traditional cuisine practised by Indians at home but the particularly interesting and distinctive variety that is served in Indian restaurants all over the world.

THE VEGETARIAN CURRY

Ideal for all who love Indian food but wish to avoid meat. This book by Asha Naran contains traditional recipes that are easy to follow, using ingredients that are readily available. Full descriptions of the dishes are included, along with serving suggestions and suggested menus.

AN INDIAN HOUSEWIFE'S RECIPE BOOK

Simple, economical family recipes made from ingredients and spices which are widely available. Not only are curries featured, but there is an array of starters, snacks, raitas, chutneys, pickles and sweets. Everything, in fact, that characterizes Indian cookery for people all over the world.

RIGHT WAY
PUBLISHING POLICY

HOW WE SELECT TITLES
RIGHT WAY consider carefully every deserving manuscript. Where an author is an authority on his subject but an inexperienced writer, we provide first-class editorial help. The standards we set make sure that every **RIGHT WAY** book is practical, easy to understand, concise, informative and delightful to read. Our specialist artists are skilled at creating simple illustrations which augment the text wherever necessary.

CONSISTENT QUALITY
At every reprint our books are updated where appropriate, giving our authors the opportunity to include new information.

FAST DELIVERY
We sell **RIGHT WAY** books to the best bookshops throughout the world. It may be that your bookseller has run out of stock of a particular title. If so, he can order more from us at any time – we have a fine reputation for "same day" despatch, and we supply any order, however small (even a single copy), to any bookseller who has an account with us. We prefer you to buy from your bookseller, as this reminds him of the strong underlying public demand for **RIGHT WAY** books. Readers who live in remote places, or who are housebound, or whose local bookseller is unco-operative, can order direct from us by post.

FREE
If you would like an up-to-date list of all **RIGHT WAY** titles currently available, please send a stamped self-addressed envelope to

ELLIOT RIGHT WAY BOOKS,
KINGSWOOD, SURREY, KT20 6TD, U.K.